The impact of enforcement on street users in England

This publication can be provided in other formats, such as large print, Braille and audio. Please contact: Communications, Joseph Rowntree Foundation, The Homestead, 40 Water End, York YO30 6WP Tel: 01904 615905 Email: info@jrf.org.uk

Available in other formats

The impact of enforcement on street users in England

Sarah Johnsen and Suzanne Fitzpatrick

JOSEPH ROWNTREE
FOUNDATION

First published in Great Britain in 2007 by

The Policy Press
Fourth Floor, Beacon House
Queen's Road
Bristol BS8 1QU
UK

Tel no   +44 (0)117 331 4054
Fax no   +44 (0)117 331 4093
Email   tpp-info@bristol.ac.uk
www.policypress.org.uk

© University of York 2007

Transferred to Digital Print 2007

Published for the Joseph Rowntree Foundation by The Policy Press

ISBN 978 1 84742 001 5

British Library Cataloguing in Publication Data
A catalogue record for this book is available from the British Library.

Library of Congress Cataloging-in-Publication Data
A catalog record for this book has been requested.

Sarah Johnsen is a research fellow in the Centre for Housing Policy and **Suzanne Fitzpatrick** is Director of the Centre for Housing Policy, University of York.

The **Joseph Rowntree Foundation** has supported this project as part of its programme of research and innovative development projects, which it hopes will be of value to policy makers, practitioners and service users. The facts presented and views expressed in this report are, however, those of the authors and not necessarily those of the Foundation.

The statements and opinions contained within this publication are solely those of the authors and not of the University of Bristol or The Policy Press. The University of Bristol and The Policy Press disclaim responsibility for any injury to persons or property resulting from any material published in this publication.

The Policy Press works to counter discrimination on grounds of gender, race, disability, age and sexuality.

Cover photograph supplied by www.third-avenue.co.uk
Cover design by Qube Design Associates, Bristol
Printed and bound by CPI Group (UK) Ltd, Croydon, CR0 4YY

Contents

Acknowledgements

We are greatly indebted to all of the people who participated in this research, from Southwark, Westminster, Brighton, Leeds, Birmingham and Camden. In particular, we would like to thank the 66 former or current street users who shared their experiences with us in in-depth interviews and focus groups.

We are also grateful to the Joseph Rowntree Foundation for supporting this work, and in particular Theresa McDonagh and Katharine Knox, who managed the project on the Foundation's behalf and, as always, provided us with excellent support and guidance. *The Big Issue in the North* Trust initiated this research, and we would like to record our thanks to Fay Selvan, who prompted us to undertake this study, and Alison Watson, who provided support, encouragement and practical assistance throughout the research process.

The project advisory group offered us both valuable advice and practical help that greatly eased the research process. The members were as follows:

Gary Messenger, Department for Communities and Local Government

Maureen Noble and Ian Deasha, both of Manchester City Council

Andy Pritchard, West Midlands Police

Paul Rice, Manchester City Centre Management Company

Julie Robinson, St Anne's Shelter and Housing Action

Fay Selvan, *The Big Issue in the North*

Garry Shewen, Cheshire Police

Jeremy Swain, Thames Reach

Jean Templeton, St Basils

Evelyn Tehrani, Crisis

Nicholas Pleace (Centre for Housing Policy, University of York) undertook some of the fieldwork for this study, and offered detailed comments on the draft report. Steve Povey (Shelter Cymru) provided us with very helpful advice on the legal material contained in this report. We would also like to thank Claire Luscombe (The Salvation Army) for her valuable feedback on the draft report.

All opinions and any errors contained in the report are, as always, the sole responsibility of the authors.

Summary

Street homelessness has been a policy priority in England since the early 1990s, and there has been a substantial subsequent decline in levels of rough sleeping. However, concerns have mounted in recent years about the 'problematic street culture' sometimes associated with rough sleeping – especially begging and street drinking – and there has been a significant shift towards enforcement interventions aimed at the 'street users' involved in these activities. The enforcement and coercive measures taken against street users include Anti-Social Behaviour Orders (ASBOs); injunctions; arrests for begging or sleeping rough under the 1824 Vagrancy Act; controlled drinking zones; dispersal orders; designing out; and alternative giving schemes.

The main aim of this research project was to evaluate the impact of these enforcement interventions on the welfare of street users in England. The key objectives were as follows:

- to identify the range of enforcement interventions currently undertaken to address 'street culture' in England;
- to explore the extent to which enforcement action is linked to supportive interventions;
- to assess the overall impact of enforcement interventions on the welfare of (current and former) street users;
- to identify the circumstances associated with any particular positive or negative outcomes of enforcement action;
- to assess the impact of enforcement measures on other stakeholders in the local community, and in particular residents and businesses.

The research comprised an in-depth evaluation of the impact of enforcement interventions in five case study areas across England: Westminster, Southwark, Birmingham, Leeds and Brighton. Across these, a total of 66 (former or current) 'street users' participated in the research: 37 in in-depth interviews and a further 29 in focus groups. In addition, 82 'support providers' and 'enforcement agents' were interviewed, as were 27 local residents and business proprietors.

This study confirmed the findings of previous research that those involved in street activities were highly vulnerable individuals: almost all street users encountered had substance misuse problems, many had mental health problems, and the great majority had suffered a traumatic childhood. All of the in-depth interviewees were homeless or had a history of homelessness.

It was mainly local rather than national pressures that led to a shift towards the use of enforcement in the case study areas, although central government played a key role in providing the 'tools' to enable action to be taken. Begging, and street drinking in large groups, were perceived by local residents and businesses to have had a very negative impact within concentrated areas in each of the case studies. Affected members of the public, and enforcement agents, were not unsympathetic to the vulnerability of street users, but were clear that their top priority was a reduction in the negative impact of street culture on their daily lives. Most felt that the strategies adopted in their local area had been successful in bringing about a sharp decline in street activities.

'Harder' forms of enforcement – particularly ASBOs – were key to the reduction of street activities in targeted areas and clearly had a powerful (direct and indirect) deterrent effect. While far fewer ASBOs had actually been issued to street users than was commonly supposed, it was clear that even the threat of an ASBO could bring about substantial changes in street behaviour because of the possibility of long prison sentences for breach of ASBO conditions.

Moreover, when preceded by warning stages (such as Acceptable Behaviour Contracts [ABCs]), and integrated with intensive supportive interventions, ASBOs could bring about positive benefits for some street users – causing them to desist from anti-social behaviour (ASB) and engage with drug treatment and other services. Enforcement in these instances acted as a 'crisis point' prompting reflection and change.

However, the degree to which hard enforcement measures were accompanied by supportive interventions was highly variable across the case studies. In some areas carefully coordinated support packages were integral to enforcement strategies; in others, enforcement and supportive interventions were employed virtually independently of one another.

Some of the 'softer' forms of enforcement – especially controlled drinking zones and environmental designing out measures – were highly effective in reducing the visibility of street activities. However, such measures rarely provided any discernible benefits for street users themselves.

Enforcement (in both its hard and soft forms) clearly led to 'geographical displacement' (relocation of street activities), and there was also consistent evidence of 'activity displacement', wherein street users turned to shoplifting, for example, during 'begging clampdowns', in order to generate the funds required for their drug and/or alcohol problem.

While it is impossible to predict with certainty what the outcomes of enforcement will be for a given individual or group, it is clear that the impact depends to a significant degree on the local policy and practice context. In particular, 'positive' responses by street users to enforcement action were far likelier where these measures were integrated with intensive support, and where there was appropriate interagency working.

Also crucial are the personal circumstances of an individual street user. Those most likely to respond positively to enforcement had something positive to return or aspire to, and/or had experienced other recent 'crisis points' (such as an overdose scare, or the death of a friend) that had prompted them to contemplate their lifestyle and future. Conversely, street users were less likely to benefit from enforcement if, for example, they had a long history of street living and/or substance misuse, had inadequately treated mental health problems, already had an extensive criminal record, or considered themselves to be 'hopeless cases'.

Given the unpredictability of outcomes for specific street users, and the potential for very negative impacts for some (for example, diversion into more dangerous activities/spaces as well as the possibility of lengthy prison sentences), enforcement is undoubtedly a *high risk* strategy with regards to the well-being of street users.

A key policy implication arising from this analysis included the importance of addressing gaps within local service networks, not only to increase the likelihood of successful resettlement and treatment of drug or alcohol addictions, but also to enhance the incentive for street users to move away from lifestyles that are damaging to themselves and, sometimes, to the local community. While access to drug treatment has improved significantly in many areas in recent years, provision of alcohol treatment services remains inadequate, and the availability of appropriate treatment for mental health problems is frequently poor.

Also, the specific actions and personal circumstances of street users must be taken into account in making a considered judgement on whether enforcement action is both necessary and likely to be effective in each particular case. 'Blanket' enforcement policies are inappropriate. Harder enforcement measures (for example, ASBOs) should only be used as a last resort, after appropriate 'warning stages', and should never be used with extremely vulnerable street users, particularly those with serious mental health problems.

For enforcement to have a reasonable prospect of prompting a positive response from any street users, it must always be carefully integrated with individually tailored and (immediately) accessible supportive interventions; involve effective interagency working; and be articulated in such a way as to emphasise the positive options open to a street user, particularly the availability of appropriate accommodation and support.

Introduction

Background to the study

Street homelessness has been a policy priority in England since the early 1990s (Fitzpatrick et al, 2000; May et al, 2005), and subsequent years saw a substantial decline in levels of rough sleeping as a result of the work of the Rough Sleepers Initiative (RSI) and, especially, the Rough Sleepers Unit (RSU) (Randall and Brown, 2002). Significant additional resources have been devoted to addressing the accommodation and support needs of rough sleepers, and at the same time the government has made clear its wish to "improve the incentives to come inside" by challenging traditional street-based services that they viewed as sustaining homelessness (ODPM, 1999).

Concerns have mounted over the past few years about 'street culture' activities associated with rough sleeping, especially begging and street drinking. The evidence is now overwhelming that begging (in the UK) is very closely associated with alcohol and drug misuse, and also that the great majority of those involved are 'homeless',[1] with around half to three quarters sleeping rough at the point of interview in all relevant studies, and virtually all of the remainder living in hostels or other forms of insecure or temporary accommodation (Danczuk, 2000; Fitzpatrick and Kennedy, 2000; Vision 21, 2000; Jowett et al, 2001). While all of these existing reports are now several years old, our research findings are consistent with these earlier findings regarding both the housing status and substance misuse profile of people involved in street activities (see below). Likewise, our work confirms earlier evidence that most of those involved in street activities, particularly begging, have suffered extremely traumatic life histories (Fitzpatrick and Kennedy, 2000). The impact of street activities on the public living or working in 'hotspot' areas has been the predominant policy concern (Fooks and Pantazis, 1999), although research has also highlighted the potentially exploitative nature of relationships between 'street users' (Ballantyne, 1999; see also Allen et al, 2003).

In 2003, the Home Office's Anti-Social Behaviour Unit (ASBU) (since replaced by the Respect Task Force) took up the mantle of 'problem street culture', with begging in particular becoming the target for a range of interventions (Davies and Waite, 2004). Begging was already a crime in England under the 1824 Vagrancy Act, and became a 'recordable' offence in December 2003, meaning that community sentences could be imposed on conviction. The Anti-Social Behaviour Action Plan, published in October 2003, introduced targeted action to reduce begging and other aspects of problem street culture in 30 criminal justice intervention programme areas, with plans to significantly reduce begging in five 'trailblazer' local authorities (Home Office, 2002). Enforcement measures used against those begging in these trailblazer areas (and elsewhere) include criminal sanctions, Anti-Social Behaviour Orders (ASBOs) and injunctions, often in combination

---

[1] As used in this report, the term 'homeless' is used to describe an individual who is sleeping rough or otherwise lacks settled accommodation. This therefore includes those in temporary or insecure forms of accommodation such as hostels, night shelters, Bed and Breakfast hotels, squats, or who are staying temporarily with family or friends.

with 'alternative giving schemes'. Street drinking has also been the focus of concerted action, such that by August 2006, 177 local authorities in England had restricted the outdoor consumption of alcohol within their jurisdictions via a Designated Public Places Order (DPPO) (Crime Reduction, 2006) (see below for further details on DPPOs).

This shift towards enforcement in street culture policies is not unique to England, but is evident across much of the US (Fischer, 1992; Mitchell, 1997; Snow and Mulcahy, 2001; National Coalition for the Homeless, 2004), and many other cities in economically developed nations have taken action against those involved in rough sleeping and/or begging, including Japan (Malinas, 2004), Germany (Eick, 2003) and Belgium (Adriaenssens and Cle, 2006). What marks England out as different, however, is the extent of central government support and encouragement for enforcement action to address street culture – in most other countries enforcement initiatives have been entirely locally driven.

Key enforcement interventions

There are a wide range of enforcement measures now at the disposal of the police and local authorities to tackle street culture in England. The main types of measures utilised are defined and explained below, beginning with what might be termed the 'harder' forms of enforcement and moving on to the 'softer' (generally less forceful or coercive) interventions employed. This broad structure is not, however, intended to suggest that these interventions can be arranged along a strict 'continuum' of severity.

ASBOs: introduced by the 1998 Crime and Disorder Act, ASBOs are civil orders intended to protect the public from behaviour that causes, or is likely to cause, 'harassment, alarm or distress'. These orders contain conditions prohibiting an offender from specific anti-social acts ('behavioural' conditions) and/or entering defined areas ('geographical' conditions), and are effective for a minimum period of two years. Local authorities, the police and registered social landlords (RSLs) can apply for ASBOs. The two main types are 'stand-alone' ASBOs (granted by the civil courts) and 'post-conviction' ASBOs (granted after sentencing on a criminal case, and also sometimes known as CRASBOs). Hearsay evidence is admissible in all ASBO hearings, but there must be a criminal standard of evidence ('beyond all reasonable doubt') that the defendant has acted in an anti-social manner in the past. Breach of an ASBO is a criminal offence (requiring criminal standards of proof), with a maximum penalty of five years' imprisonment. 'Interim ASBOs' can be granted pending a full ASBO hearing, where there is sufficient evidence of an urgent need to protect the public. Since July 2005, such interim ASBOs are now available 'post-conviction' in the same way as in 'stand-alone' applications. These temporary orders are made for a fixed period, but attract the same penalties for breach as full ASBOs while in effect.

Acceptable Behaviour Contracts (ABCs) (and Acceptable Behaviour Agreements [ABAs]) are written agreements between a person involved in anti-social behaviour (ASB) and agencies – such as the police, local authorities or RSLs – defining acceptable standards of behaviour that the person agrees to abide by. The ABC/ABA is an informal procedure but often has legal implications as 'breach' of conditions may be used as evidence to support an ASBO application. Similarly, various forms of 'warning letter' are sometimes issued by the police and local authorities as early intervention devices, designed to prevent the need to proceed to an ASBO application.

Injunctions: the 1972 Local Government Act (Section 222) enables local authorities to apply for injunctions against behaviour that is a public nuisance. The 2003 Anti-Social Behaviour Act allows for the power of arrest to be attached to such injunctions where the behaviour complained of involves violence, threats of violence or a risk of harm. Breach of civil injunctions can result in a prison sentence, provided appropriate warnings are given.

1824 Vagrancy Act: this legislation specifies that both begging (Section 3) and persistent begging (Section 4) are arrestable offences. As noted above, begging is now a 'recordable' offence, and so the details of those convicted are recorded on the Police National Computer.[2] The Vagrancy Act (Section 4) also makes it an offence to sleep rough, but only where it can be shown that an individual has been directed to a 'free' place of shelter and has failed to take this up. None of these are imprisonable offences: the maximum penalty on conviction is a fine.

Controlled drinking zones: the consumption of alcohol has been restricted in many public places by byelaws[3] or DPPOs, the latter being introduced by the 2001 Criminal Justice and Police Act. While it is not an offence to consume alcohol within a designated area, the police can require a person drinking to stop, and can confiscate the alcohol of anyone who is either drinking in the designated area or whom they believe intends to do so (a practice commonly referred to as 'de-canning'). The 2003 Licensing Act extended police powers to confiscate unopened as well as opened vessels. Individuals failing to comply with police requests to stop drinking, or to surrender their alcohol, can be arrested and fined.

Dispersal Orders: the 2003 Anti-Social Behaviour Act (Section 30) enables the police to issue group Dispersal Orders requiring people to disperse in a public designated place. It is a criminal offence to refuse to comply with such an Order.

Designing out: this is manipulation of the built environment to make 'hotspots' of street activity less habitable for street users (by, for example, removing seating regularly occupied by street drinkers). 'Hotspot closure' was a term used in some case studies to refer to a more carefully coordinated and phased approach, with close involvement of support agencies, to move people on from areas of concentrated street activity.

Alternative giving schemes or diverted giving campaigns: these typically involve publicity campaigns to discourage the public from giving directly to those begging, together with the provision of donation boxes in town or city centre locations, and the distribution of proceeds to local homelessness charities.

---

[2] While the designation of begging as a recordable offence meant that community sentences became available on conviction, including Drug Treatment and Testing Orders (DTTOs), in practice we found that DTTOs had not been used in cases of begging in our case studies, so are not discussed in this report.

[3] As of 31 August 2006 all remaining relevant byelaws were converted by operation of law to DPPOs.

Study aims

The main aim of this research project was to evaluate the impact of this range of enforcement interventions on 'street users' in England. The specific objectives were as follows:

- to identify the range of enforcement interventions currently undertaken to address 'street culture' in England;
- to explore the extent to which enforcement action is linked to supportive interventions;
- to assess the overall impact of enforcement interventions on the welfare of (current and former) street users;
- to identify the circumstances associated with any particular positive or negative outcomes of enforcement action;
- to assess the impact of enforcement measures on other stakeholders in the local community, and in particular residents and businesses.

The main groups of street users focused on were people sleeping rough, people involved in begging and street drinkers, all of whom have been subject to enforcement interventions (Fitzpatrick and Jones, 2005). *The Big Issue* (street magazine) vendors have been caught up in enforcement initiatives in some areas, so some consideration was also given to how they had been affected. It should be noted that the terms 'street users', 'street lifestyles', 'street activities', 'street populations' and 'street culture' are often used interchangeably in policy documents and by those working in this field, and thus all of these terms are employed in this report.

The Big Issue in the North Trust initiated and participated in this research because they were concerned that enforcement action was escalating in England without an adequate assessment of its impact on street users, many of whom, as noted above, are known to be highly vulnerable (Fitzpatrick and Kennedy, 2000). The research was conducted by the Centre for Housing Policy (CHP), at the University of York, which had complete intellectual and methodological control over the study's conduct and reporting.

Research methods

There were three stages to the research.

Stage 1 comprised a review of existing research and 'grey literature', including policy statements and other relevant documents published by central government departments (for example, Home Office, Office of the Deputy Prime Minister, and Department for Environment, Food and Rural Affairs), local authorities, and major homelessness agencies. This exercise set the context for the study, including the background section above, and was an essential step in selecting potential case studies for Stage 2.

It was also intended that Stage 1 of the study would involve compiling all quantitative information available at the national level on the use of enforcement measures against street users. However, little data collected at national level was useful for this purpose, often because it did not distinguish between street users and other 'offenders'. Detailed statistics at the local level, where available, are reported for each of the case study areas (see below).

Stage 2 comprised an in-depth evaluation of the impact of enforcement interventions in five case study areas across England. The selection aimed to capture the range of relevant policy and implementation approaches across the main geographical contexts within which street culture was viewed as an ongoing problem, including some of the anti-begging trailblazer authorities. The case study areas chosen were as follows:

- Westminster (an anti-begging trailblazer)
- Southwark
- Birmingham
- Leeds (an anti-begging trailblazer)
- Brighton (an anti-begging trailblazer).

In addition, a small amount of fieldwork was conducted in Camden, as their approach to tackling street culture emerged as of great interest during the other London fieldwork.

The fieldwork undertaken in each of the five case study areas included the following:

Analysis of available quantitative data on enforcement actions and outcomes

Data was collected, where available, on the use of the following enforcement interventions:

- ASBOs for begging, street drinking or other street culture activities (including information on numbers granted, breaches, prison sentences for breach, ABCs, warning letters or similar);
- civil injunctions for begging, street drinking, or other street culture activities;
- arrests for begging;
- Dispersal Orders aimed at street users;
- arrests for rough sleeping;
- contraventions of controlled drinking zones (by street drinkers).

Interviews with key informants and frontline workers

Interviewees included those in policy or strategic positions in the local area, and frontline workers from a range of services. Some of these interviews were conducted on a one-to-one basis, and others were conducted in small focus groups. Among those interviewed were:

- 'support providers', for example, accommodation providers, outreach workers, drug and alcohol workers, health service professionals and resettlement workers;
- 'enforcement agents', for example, police officers, magistrates, probation officers, ASB officers, city centre managers, and (other) local authority representatives.

Across all five case studies, a total of 82 'support providers' and 'enforcement agents' participated in the research. Details are provided in Appendix A.

Interviews with current and former street users

In each case study in-depth interviews and focus groups were conducted with current and former street users, selected to represent the range of experience of enforcement in that locality. In total, 66 current or former street users participated in the research: 37 in the in-depth interviews, and a further 29 in the focus groups. Again, see Appendix A for details.

The in-depth interviews were an especially important element of the research because these allowed us to investigate street users' experiences in detail in order to analyse the impact and interconnections between the different types of interventions they had encountered. As this was a qualitative study, the interviewees were selected purposively, to capture key dimensions of the experience of enforcement, and were thus not intended to be statistically representative of the population of street users as a whole (a population whose precise parameters are in any case ill-defined).

However, it is important to note that the broad profile and characteristics of these 37 in-depth interviewees matched what would be expected from previous research among the street population (for example, Arlington Housing Association, 1992; Shimwell, 1999; Fitzpatrick and Kennedy, 2000; Alcohol Concern, 2001; Jowett et al, 2001; Randall and Brown, 2006). Thus the great majority of the sample was male (only five were female), and all were white British. The largest group were in their 30s (16 interviewees), with six each in their 20s, 40s and 50s, and only one interviewee in their late teens and one in their 60s. All bar one had, or had had, a drug and/or alcohol problem, with several also reporting serious mental health problems. The great majority had had childhoods disrupted by traumatic events, such as parental divorce, death of a parent, physical or sexual abuse, parental drug problems, and/or experience of local authority care. There were a small number who reported happy and stable childhoods, followed by a crisis in adulthood that led to their substance misuse, homelessness and involvement in street culture.

Given the controversy over this issue (for a review, see Fitzpatrick and Jones, 2005), it is important to highlight that three quarters of the in-depth interview sample (27 interviewees) were homeless at the point of interview: 10 were sleeping rough, 11 were living in hostels, rolling/night shelters or Bed and Breakfast hotels, five were 'sofa-surfing' round friends and relatives and one was staying in a squat. All of the 10 interviewees who had settled accommodation at the point of interview had a history of homelessness.

Many of the in-depth interviewees had criminal records, usually for repeated minor offences. Out of the 37, 12 had received ASBOs for street culture activities, but none had had civil injunctions granted against them. Eighteen had been arrested for begging and three had been arrested for sleeping rough. Experience of the 'softer' forms of enforcement – police cautions, being moved on or 'de-canned' in controlled drinking zones – was widespread.

Interviews with local residents and business proprietors

While the primary interest of this study was the impact of enforcement on street users, it was also crucial to take account of the perspectives of other members of the local community. Thus a range of local residents and business proprietors participated in the research: 27 in total across all of the case studies. The manner of their involvement depended on what was most convenient for them and appropriate in the context, so in some cases focus group discussions were conducted, in others one-to-one or telephone interviews were employed.

Other activities

Wherever possible, a member of the research team attended multiagency ASB operational forums, and/or accompanied street outreach workers or dedicated street community police officers on their usual 'rounds' within the case studies.

Stage 3 of the research involved 'feedback seminars' in each of the five case study locations when the final report was ready in draft form, in order to:

- confirm the factual content regarding each case study;
- test the recommendations against experience;
- introduce a (limited) longitudinal element into the study by providing the opportunity to check on the position in the case studies at the end of the project;
- 'give something back' to those who had assisted with the research.

Analytical process

All interviews were recorded where interviewees gave their consent. Most of the key informant in-depth interviews, as well as the focus groups with street users, frontline workers and the wider community, were written up in a 'notes and quotes' format. Several of the most interesting and/or detailed of such interviews were fully transcribed. All of this material was then analysed using a shared thematic framework. All of the in-depth interviews with street users were recorded (where interviewees consented), and these recordings were fully transcribed and analysed using a shared thematic framework.

Where interviews could not be recorded, for reasons of practicality or consent, contemporaneous notes were taken during the interview and written up immediately afterwards. This was relevant to only a small number of interviews across the case studies.

Evaluative approach

This was a predominantly qualitative rather than quantitative evaluation of the impact of enforcement action on street users. For both practical and ethical reasons, it is difficult to conduct an experimental evaluation (using randomised control trials) in a field such as this, and some would argue that this is in any case inappropriate because it eliminates the context so crucial in determining *why* certain outcomes are achieved (or not) by interventions. Thus we instead undertook a 'realistic evaluation', whereby the focus is not so much on quantifying the effects of an intervention as on investigating: "What works, for whom, in what circumstances" (Pawson and Tilley, 1997, p 85).

We started from the premise that involvement in street culture is problematic because of the strong evidence that these activities are highly damaging to those involved. Numerous research studies demonstrate the humiliation, violence, abuse and poor health endured by people who experience rough sleeping, begging, street drinking and other associated street activities (MHF, 1996; Pleace and Quilgars, 1996; Ballantyne, 1999; Fitzpatrick and Kennedy, 2000). As noted above, research has also indicated the traumatic life histories typically experienced by those who become involved in any or all of these activities.

Thus, we also take the view that social justice demands that any interventions designed to minimise or eradicate street activities should, on balance at least, be beneficial rather than damaging to this vulnerable group (Fitzpatrick and Jones, 2005). At the same time, the impact of these activities on other members of the community must be given due regard in assessing the overall appropriateness and justice of interventions, particularly where street activities have a major impact on particular sections of the community.

Within the parameters set by these broad (value-based) assumptions (Nagel, 1986), and to the best of our abilities, this research was conducted with an open mind as to the impacts, utility and justice of enforcement interventions.

Report structure

The next chapter reviews the key drivers for enforcement across the case studies, and presents a detailed account of the development and implementation of enforcement interventions in each of these locations. Chapter 3 then moves on to consider the perspectives of all research participants on whether enforcement action on street culture is, overall, justified and effective, and Chapter 4 provides an in-depth analysis of the merits and demerits of specific enforcement interventions. Chapter 5 summarises our evidence on the circumstances (both policy and personal) that make it more or less likely that enforcement action will have a positive impact on the well-being of targeted street users. Chapter 6 presents the overall conclusions and recommendations from the research.

2

The case studies: local experience of developing and implementing enforcement interventions

Introduction

This chapter details the development, implementation and impacts of enforcement interventions in each of the case study areas. Consistent themes could be discerned across all of the case studies with regards to the local pressures that prompted a shift towards enforcement, and these issues are considered first, before in-depth consideration is given to the strategies adopted to combat street culture in individual case study areas.

Origins: the impact of street culture on the local community

Concerns about the impact of 'street culture' on town and city centres have a long history in the UK (Wardhaugh, 1996). While the recent step change in street population policies across England lies in part in central government efforts to promote enforcement (as well as supportive) action in this area, local rather than national pressures appeared to be the predominant factor driving policy change across our case studies.

In this respect it is important to bear in mind that, while the numbers of rough sleepers reduced significantly in most city centres after the work of the Rough Sleepers Initiative and Rough Sleepers Unit, there remained highly visible concentrations of street activities in specific localities. This was the case in all five of our case studies, with concern among local residents and businesses reported to be founded on the number of people begging in the city centre and/or the size and visibility of 'drinking schools' (groups of street drinkers) in specific areas, and the potential danger to public health and safety presented by environmental 'pollution' associated with street lifestyles (particularly human waste and the inappropriate disposal of used hypodermic needles).

There was also sometimes thought to have been a deterioration in the behaviour of those involved in street culture, particularly an increase in aggressive begging and/or increased noise and displays of aggression within large congregations of people drinking outdoors. Some support providers and enforcement agents attributed these perceived changes in the nature of street activity to the recent dramatic increase in crack cocaine use (Turning

Point, 2005), and/or the increase in methadone prescription and boredom subsequently experienced by former heroin users that has contributed to an increase in the consumption of alcohol or other drugs 'on top':

> 'There's a much much greater use of drugs and alcohol together.... That has completely changed and most people are using anything they can get their hands on now. It's complete poly drug use and much more chaotic behaviour and lifestyles.' (service provider, Leeds)

These local concerns about street culture tended to be greatest where a number of factors coalesced to facilitate the congregation of large groups of street users, including:

- the geographical concentration of services (for example, hostels, day centres, drug treatment centres);
- a built environment conducive to street lifestyles (for example, overhangs providing shelter);
- proximity to illicit street drug markets and/or begging opportunities (for example, tourist attractions);
- the diversion of police attention towards more serious criminal activity (for example, prevention of terrorism after the bombings in central London in July 2005).

It was clear that members of the public we interviewed considered some aspects of street culture more objectionable than others. People sleeping rough were most likely to be viewed with compassion given the obvious discomfort of their situation and common assumption that they must have 'fallen on hard times'. While people begging were often viewed as less threatening than street drinkers, they were still a cause for concern because of their drug-related 'deviance'. Street drinkers have a less 'taboo' addiction than drug users, but were more likely to be in large groups, and to be loud and 'rowdy', particularly later in the day as they become more inebriated:

> 'It's like being in the worst pub that you could imagine, in the worst side of town. You just wouldn't want to go in there. You've got people wandering around half cut at all times of day.' (business proprietor, Southwark)

Where street activity was highly concentrated in specific residential areas it could create environments that felt highly intimidating for those living in the immediate vicinity:

> 'The square was taken over by street drinkers.... It became very unpleasant to live around here, effectively.... They were totally anti-social. I mean they drink, litter, urinate and worse in public.... Something had to be done about it because it was just unbearable.... You were looking over your shoulder when you were coming in and out because they're there all the time, they're watching you. You're worried about your kids, people coming over.' (resident, Brighton)

Related to these concerns about intimidation, business proprietors expressed a strong conviction that the presence of street users deterred potential customers from entering their shops:

> '[Begging] actually puts people off and turns people away. You'll actually see people make a diversion to go away from them and that possibly actually turns people away from our store.' (shop proprietor, Leeds)

Concerns voiced by members of the local community were usually founded on a *fear* of threat or danger rather than personal experience of verbal or physical abuse from street users:

> 'There's some people who do beg who we know are also drug users and there's something about that culture that I find quite scary ... because they've got an addiction I don't know what they'd do for the money. So if we're talking a late night scenario and I'm by myself and they ask me for money and I say no, potentially that could escalate. I mean it never *has* happened and I don't really think it would.... It's potential fear I s'pose.' (business proprietor, Leeds)

Several support providers and police officers commented that, while incidences of verbal abuse and/or physical violence are not uncommon *within* the street population – particularly among street drinkers – such expressions of aggression are only very rarely directed at members of the wider public:

> '... they're quite an 'ugly' bunch as it were. But I think the public really had very little to fear from them because, yes, they were involved in criminality, but that criminality would be shoplifting and drug misuse.... If it was things like assault or disturbances, invariably it would be amongst themselves and wouldn't involve a third party.' (police representative, Southwark)

That said, it should be noted that a small number of members of the public interviewed had been direct recipients of aggressive or threatening behaviour by street users. Thus, while community fears may well be heightened by an instinctive fear of those who are visibly 'different', they are not groundless.

It was clear that a combination of local concerns, together with the provision of new legal and policy 'tools' from a sympathetic central government, led to a shift towards enforcement in each of the case study areas. The precise nature and form of enforcement actions differed across these case studies, as now discussed. Please note that the accounts presented below relate to developments up until the point when the fieldwork was carried out (the majority of which was conducted between September 2005 and March 2006). The range of statistics available on relevant enforcement actions and their impacts varied across the case studies, and thus the accounts presented below are somewhat uneven in this respect.

Southwark: 'escalating enforcement'

Street population issues in Southwark comprised: street drinking in the Camberwell area (in the south of the borough), and rough sleeping and begging (with pockets of street drinking) in the north of the borough.

South of the borough: Camberwell street drinkers

Camberwell has a long historical association with street drinking, linked in part to having been a long-standing node of service provision for vulnerable people. Residents had exhibited a degree of tolerance of street drinking for many years, but this began to diminish when the number of drinkers congregating on Camberwell Green in particular was seen to escalate. A local mapping and intelligence gathering exercise identified a street drinking population of 150 named individuals, with a core group of 30-40 who were present on a daily basis. There was unanimous agreement by all interviewed that "something needed to be done" given the scale of the problem.

A partnership, spearheaded by the Community Safety Partnership (CSP) team, and including both enforcement agencies and support providers, was set up in 2004 to devise a strategy and the council funded additional support services including outreach services and 'wet slots' at a local day centre. A system of 'escalating enforcement' was then utilised, which involved requesting street users to sign an ABC if they had come to notice for ASB in relation to street drinking more than four times in a month. A total of 20 individuals signed ABCs. Street drinkers were given a 'breathing space' of three to six months to begin addressing their behaviour before ASBOs were pursued. Their activities were monitored by means of bi-weekly multiagency case conference meetings (attended by representatives of the Metropolitan Police, CSP, the local ASBU, wardens, outreach workers and treatment providers) that agreed an action plan for individual street users. Numbers and activity were monitored with the aid of 'visual audits', and via an innovative 'radiolink' scheme, which linked local businesses, day centres and drug treatment services to the police.

Out of a total of 20 ABCs, only six resulted in an ASBO. Four of the six ASBOs were breached: one individual was fined, and the other three served prison sentences ranging from three to five months. In a parallel process, some local off-licence licensees were successfully prosecuted, and one had their licence revoked, for persistently selling alcohol to individuals who were drunk and other associated offences.

The original target of reducing the number of drinkers by 35% was not met by the proposed date of April 2005 (the first ASBOs were only being processed at that stage), but was exceeded by December 2005 when an audit indicated that the number of drinkers had reduced by 89%. A locally commissioned evaluation indicated that street drinking had 'largely ceased' in a number of former key locations, and while still evident on Camberwell Green, was carried out in smaller groups and with less ASB (Jane Walker Consultancy Ltd, 2005). There was also a decline in anti-social incidents recorded by the police and Southwark wardens over the relevant period.

North of the borough: rough sleeping, begging and street drinking

Levels of rough sleeping have been consistently higher in the northern than in the southern parts of Southwark, concentrated especially around London Bridge and Elephant and Castle. All individuals identified as involved in street activity were discussed at monthly Operations Forum meetings, at which support providers, enforcement agencies and community organisations were represented. The process began by trying to engage rough sleepers with the St Mungo's street population outreach team (SPOT). If the Operations Forum, led by the council's Street Population and Rough Sleeping Coordinator, decided that enforcement action was needed, the council issued an ABC and behaviour was monitored. If ASB continued, then an ASBO would be pursued. This was said to happen only in extreme circumstances where behaviours were "genuinely anti-social and socially unacceptable" (local authority representative) (such as aggressive begging, public defecation/urination, leaving needles in public places). In total, 14 ABCs had been signed, leading to only three (stand-alone) ASBOs (all to people involved in begging) by September 2005.

It was noted that Southwark is relatively well endowed with hostels and supported housing projects, and the SPOT can assist rough sleepers into a wide range of services. In particular, rapid methadone 'scripting' (prescription) services have proved very successful with the most difficult and chaotic heroin users.

Local counts suggested that the number of rough sleepers had reduced significantly since 2004, and begging was down from 14 people in the Borough Market area to no more than four during weekends. That said, the central location means that there remained a fairly constant stream of newcomers and a general acceptance that street activities will never be entirely eradicated.

Westminster: 'enforcement, assistance and communication'

Unlike the other case studies, Westminster City Council did not meet its target of reducing rough sleeping by two thirds (from 1998 levels) by 2002. According to council and police representatives, homeless people arrive in the heart of the capital at a rate faster than they can be accommodated (or relocated elsewhere), and there are typically 130-150 people sleeping on the street any given night, with approximately 60 new rough sleepers identified each month.

Begging has been a major issue in the area for some time, with more than 1,300 arrests made of people begging in 2003 alone. After commissioning research into the street culture of Westminster (Vision 21, 2001), the borough's strategic response to rough sleeping was expanded to encompass 'associated street activity', including street drinking, begging and street-based drug use. Selected as an anti-begging 'trailblazer' authority in 2003, Westminster devised a three-pronged strategy focusing on:

- enforcement (to remove people begging from the streets);
- assistance (to enable people begging to change their 'disordered' lifestyles);
- communication (to deter the public from giving directly to people begging).

The Metropolitan Police Safer Streets Homeless Unit (SSHU) targeted those who were most persistent and individuals begging outside cashpoint machines. Regular 12-hour enforcement operations were also conducted wherein all people begging were arrested (regardless of whether 'passive' or 'aggressive' in style). ASB warning letters were distributed during these operations, along with a list of local support providers.

Persistent 'offenders' resident in local hostels were discussed at Target and Tasking meetings, involving the SSHU and frontline support providers. If deemed appropriate, individuals were asked to sign an ABA, on the understanding that failure to abide by the conditions could lead to an application for an ASBO. Offers of assistance via appropriate services were made throughout this process. The number of breaches allowed before proceeding to an ASBO application was individually assessed, according to an individual's behaviour and capacity to change. Where street users failed to comply, the SSHU would collate evidence and propose to the case conference that an ASBO be pursued.

As at December 2005, six ASBOs had been granted for aggressive begging in Westminster. This comparatively small number, given the scale of street activity in the borough, could be explained in part by the emphasis on the warning stages above. However, another important factor was the rejection by magistrates of ASBO applications related to persistent passive begging, on the grounds that there was insufficient evidence of 'harassment, alarm or distress'.

From July 2005 a new building based service model was adopted for the delivery of support services for street homeless people in Westminster. Although limited street outreach services were retained, this marked a shift away from traditional street-based outreach, such that rough sleepers' first point of contact typically became an officer from the SSHU or a city warden who signposted them to the nearest relevant service.

In August 2004 Westminster City Council embarked on a major public information campaign, entitled 'Killing with Kindness', in conjunction with the London Borough of Camden to discourage the public from giving money directly to people begging. An alternative giving scheme is planned for the future.

The whole of the borough was designated a controlled drinking zone in 2004, and the council's environmental team was instructed to leave pavements of designated areas wet after cleaning the streets to discourage rough sleepers from bedding down at night (a strategy known locally as 'hot-washing').

A Dispersal Order was agreed for one particular 'hotspot' in 2004, but the police rarely exercised their powers under the legislation during its six-month duration.

Local audits (conducted by the police) indicated that daytime begging had diminished, but there was a less pronounced reduction in night-time begging. Cashpoint begging had reduced dramatically, although there was some evidence to suggest that 'mobile' begging increased. Arrests for begging decreased from 89 in March 2004 (32 of which related to 'prolific beggars') to 45 in November 2004 (only three of which were 'prolific'), although these figures rose (to 56 and 7 respectively) in December of that year. A council representative reported that public complaints about begging had decreased, and that local opinion polls suggested that there has been a reduction in public concern about begging in the borough.

Brighton: 'highly targeted enforcement'

Until recently, Brighton had one of the largest recorded levels of rough sleeping outside of London, and experienced serious problems with begging and street drinking. Norfolk Square was particularly problematic – infamous as a "bastion of street drinking".

Brighton subsequently implemented the UK's first city-wide DPPO in August 2003, and was designated an anti-begging trailblazer shortly afterwards, with a target of reducing the number of people begging by 60% by March 2005.

The development of Brighton and Hove's 2004-06 Begging and Street Drinking Strategy was informed by a MORI poll in Brighton that found that people would not use a cashpoint machine if there was a person begging there and would cross the road if they saw a beggar coming. Pre-existing street outreach services were recommissioned to the Rough Sleepers Street Services Team (RSSST), which included two dedicated ASB street outreach posts (funded by the council) to work with targeted clients, who liaised very closely with Sussex police's newly developed street community policing team to put in place appropriate social care and treatment arrangements.

ASB casework forums involving police, the RSSST and a range of other voluntary sector providers were held regularly to discuss nominated individuals. Begging audits were conducted monthly, wherein police and voluntary sector workers engaged with street users and collected their personal details; this exercise was extended to incorporate a bi-monthly street drinkers audit as of April 2005.

Initial targets for intervention included those begging aggressively, street drinking school 'ringleaders', and those who were very vulnerable due to poor health. Targeting was often very precise: for example, the dedicated police team would 'look for' particular individuals and 'de-can' them (that is, confiscate their alcohol) while leaving other members of the group alone.

If a street user failed to engage adequately with the RSSST within two weeks of being identified, and continued begging or street drinking, they were referred to the ASB casework forum. Their behaviour was monitored on a monthly basis and if no improvement was apparent they were issued with an ASB warning letter. Any arrests made throughout this process were used as an opportunity for emphasising the availability of support.

Packs, including the photographs (but not names) of five targeted street drinkers, and evidence sheets for the collation of hearsay evidence on their activities, were issued to residents and traders around Norfolk Square. While some were reluctant to collate such evidence, being fearful of potential retaliation, all were assured that their anonymity would be maintained and several provided evidence for use in court. The public also played an active role in 'environmental improvements' (for example, planting gardens) to discourage street drinking in the Square.

By September 2005, there had been 42 referrals to the ASB casework forum; 14 ASBO warning letters had been issued; and 12 ASBOs had been granted (four stand-alone, eight post-conviction). All 12 ASBOs had been breached, with the resulting prison sentences ranging in length from a few weeks to two years. There were also 87 arrests for begging between June 2003 and November 2005, and 16 street drinkers had committed offences under the DPPO.

Brighton had also employed several other relevant measures. Most significantly, the local authority made it clear that it would withdraw funding from any homelessness organisations that provided services for more than an agreed two-week period to those without a proven 'local connection' to the area. The city's only 'wet' centre changed from an open-door policy to a more structured set-up, wherein only identified street drinkers could access the service. Brighton authorities were also giving consideration to re-launching an alternative giving scheme, and were considering using a Dispersal Order as an additional tool for combating street drinking.

The target for reducing begging was exceeded in Brighton – local audits indicated a 90% reduction from a baseline of 33 individuals involved, to just three over a period of 15 months from November 2003. The number of street drinking hotspots was also reduced from 18 to 5, with the remaining groups tending to be smaller, and a 56% fall was recorded in the number of identified street drinkers (from 158 to 70). In addition, there was a substantial drop in the number of complaints from the public, with no violent incidences recorded on Norfolk Square since October 2004.

Leeds: 'zero tolerance'

In 2002/03 Leeds had more identified rough sleepers than anywhere else outside of London, and was under significant pressure from central government to reduce these figures. Begging, much of which was said to be aggressive (for example, involved following people around or the odd push/shove), was reported by enforcement agents to have become a 'massive' problem. There were also concerns about 'bogus' *Big Issue* vendors (using their 'last copy' to beg).

Police intelligence indicated a strong link between a range of 'street activities', Class A drug use and other crime (including robbery). This prompted the development of a street user strategy, led by the council's Community Safety department. Leeds set a target of maintaining rough sleeper figures below 10, was an anti-begging 'trailblazer' and given the target of reducing begging by 60% by March 2005 by the Office of the Deputy Prime

Minister. No formal targets for street drinking were set, but the council was "encouraged to address it", and Leeds city centre became a DPPO.

Two new posts were created, including a street users strategic coordinator (within the Safer Leeds drugs team) and a street user proactive inspector (within the police). Weekly Target and Tasking meetings were held, involving both enforcement agencies and support providers, which typically discussed 20-30 high profile 'problematic' street user cases and aimed to facilitate their access to services and address any potential 'blocks' in service delivery. A 'street life' protocol was drawn up to improve services, signed by a range of enforcement agencies and support providers, and the council re-commissioned the rough sleepers' outreach team to include broader street population issues. Additional funding led to a rapid improvement in the provision of drug treatment services in the city, but this coincided with a reduction in availability of hostel accommodation.

The police adopted a 'zero tolerance' policy on begging. Begging operations ('sweeps') were held once a month, with all those begging arrested regardless of 'style', on the grounds that a MORI poll found that members of the public felt threatened even by those begging 'passively'. Between January 2004 and December 2006, there were 301 arrests for begging (with 106 individuals arrested in total). An alternative giving scheme was also implemented in the city.

Leeds was the only case study area in which the Vagrancy Act was used to arrest people sleeping rough (although no statistics were available regarding the number of arrests made). This approach was adopted because of the apparent links between rough sleeping and street crime, and also because rough sleeper statistics were said to have indicated that "a fair number" had tenancies.

ASBOs were not pursued against those who simply slept rough, but rather with street users who were exhibiting the 'extremes' of behaviour, such as injecting in public or begging aggressively, with CCTV footage being used as evidence of such behaviour.

As at July 2006, 27 'stand-alone' ASBOs and 10 post-conviction ASBOs had been issued to street users in Leeds (it should be noted that these figures include street-based sex workers). At least 14 of these ASBOs had been breached, and five individuals had served prison sentences for breach.

(Some) members of the wider community in Leeds were informed of (most) ASBOs (after a risk assessment) via information leaflets, which included the individual's name, photograph and a list of the activities prohibited by their ASBO. In the case of ASBOs against street users, street wardens gave these leaflets to relevant local business proprietors (those directly affected by begging activity, for example) and support providers dealing with the individuals concerned.

Authorities in Leeds were considering using ABCs, but had not utilised them to date, primarily because it was felt that where a person got the point of being 'ASBOd' their chaotic lifestyles dictated that: "It had got past the stage of voluntary agreements being useful" (police representative).

Begging and rough sleeping reduction targets had both been met in Leeds: rough sleeping counts had not exceeded five for the past two years, and begging in the city centre was said to have "virtually disappeared". It was felt, however, that the problem had crept back very slightly since the diversion of police resources to deal with incidences following the London bombings.

Birmingham: 'police-led enforcement'

Five years ago, enforcement agents and some service providers considered begging a significant problem in Birmingham city centre, as were "bogus" *Big Issue* vendors engaged in the "one mag blag". Street drinking was not considered a major issue in the 'core retail area', but rather on the periphery of the city centre and in Moseley. The city's drive towards a 'cleaner, greener Birmingham' raised the profile of these concerns, and there has been a gradual move to 'harder' forms of enforcement over the past few years, with the police and city centre management largely taking the lead.

The first step taken down the enforcement 'route' was an alternative giving scheme, established in the city centre in 2003. An alcohol restricted zoning system was also established, first in the city centre and then elsewhere. The number of *Big Issue* pitches was reduced, and 'tabards' introduced to indicate that someone was a bona fide vendor. Under Birmingham's Retail Crime Initiative, people arrested for shoplifting can be 'excluded' from all participating stores in the city centre, and this was said to be a "huge disincentive for homeless people coming in to the city centre to beg or steal" (local authority representative).

In 2003 there was a failed attempt to set up a multiagency partnership – involving police, local authority and voluntary sector providers – to take forward the enforcement agenda in Birmingham. Local authority representatives commented that some voluntary sector homelessness providers had concerns about "confidentiality" issues, and were also "resistant to our ideas". There were suggestions that this may be pursued anew.

In the meantime, the police have pressed ahead with enforcement measures on street culture (especially begging) in Birmingham. 'Persistent beggars' are repeatedly arrested, with the 'pattern of arrests' used as evidence for post-conviction ASBOs (or CRASBOs). By February 2006, 12 CRASBOs had been granted for begging in Birmingham, two of which were for life. No formal statistics were available on breach, but it was said that most of those with ASBOs had 'tested the waters' by breaching it once or twice, but were now adhering to the conditions after prison sentences of one to seven months had been granted by the courts for breach.

There were no formal structures for the integration of supportive interventions with the CRASBO process in Birmingham, although there was a high degree of informal interaction between the police and some support providers with whom they had good personal relations. Likewise, interim measures – such as ABCs and ABAs – had not been used, although individuals had typically had multiple arrests for begging, and often received verbal warnings about the possibility of a CRASBO during this process.

While it was reported that more than 100 stand-alone ASBOs had been secured by the Birmingham Anti-Social Behaviour Unit (BASBU), it was not possible to identify the number attributable to 'street culture' activities. A series of warnings and supportive interventions were said to be offered before stand-alone ASBOs were pursued, but the details provided on this were vague.

Rough sleeping targets have been met (and exceeded) in Birmingham, and audits by street wardens indicate that the numbers begging have reduced. It was generally acknowledged that passive begging had been virtually eliminated in the city centre, although 'mobile' begging had probably increased.

Camden: 'carrot and stick'

Although not a full case study, there were a number of interesting dimensions of Camden's street population strategy that emerged from our limited fieldwork there. Camden's strategy was based on a 'carrot and stick' approach that aimed to improve access to services that would improve street users' quality of life while disrupting illegal and/or anti-social street activity. Multiagency Target and Tasking meetings, led by the Street Services Team (SST), developed individually tailored case plans for all street users that came to their attention as follows:

- Services were offered to street users via the SST (including targeted hostel places, ring-fenced substance misuse services and additional funding to the mental health team).
- If they failed to engage, the police issued a warning letter, and the ASB officer from the SST met with the street user to explain the impact of their activities on the community, to discuss their service needs and explain the enforcement system.
- A 'client-specific' ABA was then drawn up. As well as listing behavioural prohibitions, these stipulated the forms of support to which the recipients were entitled. This ABA stage was occasionally skipped if someone was engaged in criminal activity, or was racist or homophobic, for example.
- Each case was reviewed at a monthly Target and Tasking meeting, and a (stand-alone) ASBO was pursued if there was no change in street activity. This decision was reached in a 'consensus-driven' manner as far as possible, but as with all of the case studies that adopted multiagency approaches, council representatives had the final say in decisions to take enforcement action.

Additional funding was provided under the strategy for Operation Kingsway, a police operation to disrupt street population hotspots and collate evidence for the enforcement process.

By February 2006, of the total 207 ASBOs served in Camden, 17 were for begging and 10 were for street drinking (it is likely that there were also street users among the 70 additional individuals who received 'drug-related' ASBOs). A total of 23 SST clients had signed ABAs, with two clients refusing to sign a drafted ABA, and the behaviour of four improving so much during the drafting process that a signing was deemed unnecessary. Only four of the ABA cases progressed to a full ASBO hearing. There were no statistics available on ASBO breaches by street users, but a council representative reported that approximately 90% of breaches led to a prison sentence.

Camden's strategy was reported as having been very successful at getting providers to work in partnership, and in ensuring that clients got the services they were entitled to. Rough sleeper targets were met, and 24-hour audits indicated an 84% reduction in people begging from 96 in April 2004 to 16 in October 2005.

Conclusions

There were strong similarities across the case studies in a number of respects, particularly with regard to the nature of local pressures that prompted a shift to enforcement, and the significant impact that these measures appear to have had on overall levels of street activity, especially begging. The combination of measures employed in each case study area did vary, however, as illustrated in Table 1.

Table 1: Enforcement interventions used in each case study area

	Southwark	Westminster	Brighton	Leeds	Birmingham	Camden
ASBOs	✓	✓	✓	✓	✓	✓
ABCs/ABAs or equivalent	✓	✓	✓	✗	✗	✓
Civil injunctions	✗	✗	✓	✗	✗	✗
Arrests for begging	✓	✓	✓	✓	✓	✓
Arrests for sleeping rough	✗	✗	✗	✓	✗	✗
Controlled drinking zone	✗	✓	✓	✓	✓	✗
Dispersal Orders	✗	✓	✗	✗	✗	✗
Designing out	✓	✓	✓	✓	✓	✓
Alternative giving scheme	✓	✓	✗	✓	✓	✓

There were also important distinctions with respect to:

- the degree to which enforcement was integrated with specific and tailored offers of support;
- the availability of direct access hostel accommodation and drug, alcohol and other specialist support services in the locality;
- whether formalised processes and multiagency forums were established to structure decision making and implementation of enforcement;
- the degree of wider community involvement in, and knowledge of, the enforcement actions taken;
- whether 'stand-alone' and/or 'post-conviction' ASBOs were utilised;
- the degree to which interim measures – such as warning letters, ABCs or ABAs – were used before applying for ASBOs;
- whether ASBOs were pursued – and granted – for 'passive' begging.

The significance of this variation in local policy and practice, especially with regard to the impact on the well-being of street users, is explored in depth in subsequent chapters.

3

Perspectives on enforcement: community, enforcement agent, support provider and street user views

Introduction

This chapter examines whether enforcement approaches were, overall, considered justified and/or effective by the range of stakeholders who participated in the study, including how they defined success in this context. It begins by exploring the views of the general community (local residents and business proprietors) and enforcement agents, before examining the perspectives of support providers and street users themselves. This chapter considers research participants' *general views* regarding the use of enforcement; Chapter 4 then focuses on their opinions regarding the impacts of *specific types* of enforcement action.

Community perspectives

Given the negative impact that street culture can (and does) have on members of the public living or working in areas with concentrated street drinking or begging problems, local residents and business proprietors were typically supportive of enforcement initiatives in principle. Moreover, with few exceptions, they perceived the enforcement strategies outlined in Chapter 2 to have been effective:

> 'I think ASBOs are a good thing, to be honest. Looking at it selfishly from our perspective, it's certainly solved our problem…. The square is a different place now.' (resident, Brighton)

Members of the public were clear that the outcome they desired first and foremost was a reduction in the negative impact of street culture on their daily lives. However, most of those interviewed also expressed appreciation of, and sympathy regarding, the vulnerabilities of street users, as well as concern about the potential for enforcement measures to displace street users:

'Does it solve the problem, or does it just push them into another area? From my point of view it's good because it gets rid of them from my particular area. But whether or not it helps in general especially for themselves.... Because it's not going to stop them doing what they do if they're just going to move somewhere else and not be accounted for.' (business proprietor, Leeds)

This meant that members of the public were *most* supportive of those strategies that not only deterred individuals from anti-social street activities, but also incorporated substantial supportive interventions (see also Adler et al, 2000; Home Office, 2004).

'When I first heard about the project here ... I was a little sceptical because I thought "What's the point of just moving people on? They'll go to another area in the city, what are we achieving?"... [But] the thing that particularly impressed me was that everybody who was "targeted" ... [was] seen by a social worker, they were offered help. That was the thing that persuaded me that this was something I was happy to be involved with.' (business proprietor, Brighton)

Enforcement agent perspectives

Local enforcement agents were similarly explicit that their overriding objective in driving forward the enforcement agenda in their area was to protect the interests of the wider community:

'Some [street users] will tell you that they wish they'd never had an ASBO and it wasn't right for them. But the bottom line is it was never 'about' them, it was about the community.' (local authority representative, Camden)

They also generally felt that the enforcement strategies in their areas had been highly successful. For example, elsewhere it was noted that:

'It undid 25 years of agency malaise about a situation and location. It was fantastic. That's what ASBOs can do for you. They can just change something overnight. That and putting sloping bricks on the wall where they [street users] used to sit, simple.' (local authority representative, Brighton)

Enforcement agents emphasised that long-term interventions were required if reductions in street activity were to be sustained. Problematic street culture tended to 'creep back' whenever enforcement abated in targeted areas, as evidenced by the increase in street activity in London and Leeds when police resources were diverted away from street activity in the aftermath of the London terrorist attacks in July 2005 (see Chapter 2).

As with the wider community, it is important to stress that the enforcement agents interviewed rarely, if ever, displayed unsympathetic punitive intent. They too favoured interventions that could promote the well-being of street users, and often believed fervently that their enforcement actions had an important role to play in helping street users make positive changes in their lives:

'Another driver in Leeds was the number of drug-related deaths. And beggars and rough sleepers were a significant proportion of that number. So, some people think it's heavy enforcement for the sake of it, but it's actually rooted in concern for the individuals themselves.' (local authority representative, Leeds)

Support provider perspectives

As one might expect, support providers had far more complex and often ambivalent views regarding enforcement agendas. Many expressed concerns that councils were under pressure to 'be seen' to take action against ASB, with their clients viewed as "easy targets". Yet despite this unease, they were far from wholly opposed to the use of enforcement: on the contrary, most acknowledged the paramount need to protect the public (including other street users) from those who presented a genuine threat to the safety and well-being of people around them. Moreover, most also accepted that enforcement could engender a number of positive outcomes for their clients.

First, many support providers expressed the view that enforcement can be used as a valuable tool forcing street users to acknowledge the negative impact that street activities can have on the wider community, as well as motivating street users to engage with support services and/or desist from aspects of their lifestyle that are detrimental to their own well-being. While some frontline workers were very sceptical about the potential benefits of enforcement for their clients, others emphasised that enforcement could act as a 'lever' to push street users towards (potentially lifesaving) supportive interventions.

> 'It creates a '"window of opportunity" if it's done right. It creates periods of reflection and motivates people.' (frontline worker, Southwark)

Some support providers likened enforcement to other 'crisis points' spoken of in addiction literature that have been found to catalyse a desire to seek treatment and begin recovery (see, for example, West, 2006):

> 'We find crisis is one of the best times to offer support. And that can be the death of a friend through an overdose, it can be a near death experience that they had themselves, it could be a new health issue.... Enforcement can be the crisis.... It does sometimes work. It's crude but effective.' (support provider, Southwark)

Second, enforcement was said to act as a potential tool to help support workers break up large street drinking schools or rough sleeping encampments, which could impede the 'move-on' of their clients and enmesh newcomers in a street-based lifestyle. This strategy can also be used to undermine the influence of a group's more exploitative members:

> 'Street drinking groups are often used as camouflage for other activities. So there's a core group of street drinkers who I would define as vulnerable, non-threatening, not a risk to society generally.... If you take out the core group the peripherals ... the pimps, the street robbers, the small-time drug dealers ... don't have the cover.... So no doubt they carried on with their low-level criminality ... but they weren't able to use the street drinking group as cover and they weren't able to prey on the street drinking group.' (support provider, Southwark)

Third, and notwithstanding concerns about the availability of drugs and standards of care within prison, some support providers also noted the potential for incarceration to temporarily divorce street users from the 'chaos' of their lives outside. This can enable them to 'detoxify', to reflect on their current circumstances, and (hopefully) to contemplate their future:

> 'Sometimes the support side may be pushing for the [enforcement] because a person may actually be at risk themselves. If you've got someone begging regularly, every day, they're begging for money to fund a drug habit. They get

iller and iller.... If we've offered all the services, we need the stick approach then in order to get them into prison where they'll get treatment.' (frontline worker, Camden)

Fourth, many support providers in areas with highly coordinated enforcement strategies emphasised that one of the most positive outcomes had been associated improvements in joint working between local stakeholders. These had led to better targeting and delivery of services for a number of highly vulnerable individuals involved in street activities, many of whom had, until very recently, consistently 'fallen through' gaps in the network of service provision.

However, support providers – particularly frontline workers – also raised a number of serious concerns regarding enforcement agendas in their areas.

First, and foremost, street outreach workers (across all case studies) agreed almost unanimously that enforcement had caused many rough sleepers to 'go underground', that is, to sleep in more 'hidden' places, and displaced street drinkers and people who beg from former 'hotspots' to areas that were less heavily policed. Consequently, many had encountered difficulty locating their clients in order to offer them support. Related to this, enforcement could potentially induce what might be thought of as a 'lowest common denominator effect' – particularly acute in London – wherein if one council takes a hard stance against street culture, neighbouring authorities may feel obliged to do so as well to avoid being recipients of displaced street users:

> 'In one way it's effective because numbers are down, but at what cost? You can get numbers down if you work with the police and neighbouring boroughs don't. But if everybody did it, where do the rough sleepers go?... They're just going to get pushed into outer boroughs, and outer boroughs aren't geared up for homelessness.' (frontline worker, Westminster)

Second, there were concerns that enforcement to address begging in particular could push street users into other money-generating activities – potentially even more damaging to themselves and the rest of the community. Street users generally laid more emphasis on this point than service providers, but there was a widespread concern in Birmingham among a broad range of support agencies (including agencies who had little to do with each other, and those strongly in favour of the enforcement agenda) about a flow of young men into sex work following the clampdown on begging:

> 'We saw a significant move of our male [clients] ... that same group who were just consistently begging on the streets, moving into selling sex on the streets ... engaging in the rent scene because they're making far more money than they were through begging, and because it's much harder to make money at all through begging now than it was previously.' (support provider, Birmingham)

MATT

Aged 19, Matt had had a stable childhood until his father left when he was eight years old and his mother developed a heroin habit. He left home when he was 15, by which time he already had a heroin addiction himself, and later took crack. He said that he craved the drugs to "... give you some peace and take away the pain". He had 'sofa-surfed' (staying with different friends) and slept rough since then. Matt was heavily involved in begging and was moved on and arrested for this many times, ultimately receiving an ASBO for begging that barred him from the city centre. He had also been an occasional *Big Issue* vendor but again, since being excluded from the city centre, did not do this any more. He had not breached his ASBO but had become involved in street sex work to feed his drug habit, and claimed that this was a direct result of the restrictions imposed by his ASBO. He was not offered any support as part of the ASBO process, and was extremely bitter about the impact of the ASBO that drove him, as he saw it, into sex work. He seemed very isolated and the only support he was receiving was on an informal basis from a project worker who saw him on the street in her own time.

Third, many support providers were frustrated by the apparent failure of enforcement agencies to appreciate the vulnerability of some street users, or to take proper account of the amount of time required, and degree of support needed, to bring about sustained lifestyle changes:

> 'People's journey from the street lifestyle is not "Oh I'm going to go into a hostel or get a script" and they stop. People change over time, that's our experience.... People aren't going to walk into a hostel, throw their hands in the air and go "Hosanna I've seen the error of my ways".' (frontline worker, Southwark)

Fourth, frontline staff often encounter difficulty establishing trust with street users, and street outreach workers in particular were fearful that these fragile relationships might be jeopardised if they were perceived to be working in concert with the police. Although typically insistent that they wanted to have a 'say' in ASB operational forums (primarily to safeguard the interests of their clients), frontline workers were adamant that they should not be implicated personally in any decision to pursue enforcement lest this impede the effectiveness of their work.

Fifth, many support providers had concerns related to the effectiveness of coerced substance misuse treatment. While we did not encounter formal coerced treatment (such as DTTOs) being used to address street activities among our case studies (see Chapter 1), it is important to bear in mind that begging and street drinking revolve for the most part around drug and alcohol addiction, hence requesting street users to abstain from such activities does, in effect, equate to coercive pressure that they overcome their addiction. While drug and alcohol action team workers interviewed believed that coerced treatment is equally as 'effective' as voluntary programmes (as measured by 12-week treatment retention rates), frontline homelessness workers often argued that any attempt to 'force' a vulnerable street user into treatment is futile:

> 'You can't beat anyone with a stick to get them to deal with their drugs and alcohol. You can't beat anyone into detox if they're not ready. They're just not going to do it. It's too hard for them.' (frontline worker, Southwark)

This division of opinion mirrors an intense and ongoing debate within mainstream addiction literature. This debate revolves, primarily, around the question of whether an addict needs to have reached the 'contemplation' or 'preparation' stages in the transtheoretical model of behavioural change (see Prochaska et al, 1985; Prochaska and Vellicer, 1997) – that is, to have become aware of the impact of their addiction on themselves and others and want to undergo treatment that they recognise as being necessary for change, for treatment to be effective (see, for example, Farabee et al, 1998; Marlowe, 2001; Carver, 2004; Gregoire and Burke, 2004; Longshore et al, 2004). Thus, many scholars and practitioners question the effectiveness of coercive treatment that potentially forces addicts to 'skip' these stages and exhibit the behavioural modifications characteristic of the next, 'action', stage (that is, reduction in drug consumption). Central to this is the issue of motivation, and the extent to which external factors (such as involvement with the criminal justice system) might be transformed into internal motivation and 'readiness to change' (Checinski and Ghodse, 2004; Longshore et al, 2004).

This said, there were occasions, as noted above, where homelessness workers felt that enforcement action could act as a 'crisis' point motivating street users to engage with drug/alcohol treatment (and other services), particularly if the broader policy and personal circumstances were conducive to such a positive outcome. These contextual factors are discussed in detail in Chapter 5.

Sixth, while acknowledging the importance of protecting the public from 'genuine' ASB by street users, most support providers objected to the use of enforcement to combat the mere 'trappings' of a street lifestyle. They called for a degree of tolerance from the public regarding street users who do not 'harm' anyone, allied to a concern that ASB should not be defined by the most easily 'offended' members of society (see also Millie et al, 2005).

Seventh, and finally, many support providers expressed concern about the future of service provision within the homeless sector, fearing that resistance to local authority-led enforcement initiatives could threaten their long-term financial viability:

> 'There was a strong possibility we were going to lose some money. It was being put to us in those terms.... We were quite prepared to be pretty flexible but we don't see ourselves as part of the enforcement side of things.' (support provider)

However, it is important not to overstate this point in explaining the cooperation of voluntary sector providers in enforcement initiatives: even more key than financial pressures was a general sense that the enforcement agenda was not going to 'go away', and it was crucial to get a 'seat at the table' in order to mitigate any potential negative impacts on clients. Also, as outlined above, many support providers were, in principle, in favour of the enforcement agenda, at least where there was proper coordination with appropriately targeted supportive interventions. It was notable that the case study where there was least formal coordination – Birmingham – was also where frontline workers were most hostile to enforcement.

Street user perspectives

Street user views of enforcement reflected those of support providers in many ways. For example, they, too, were often cynical about the motives driving such initiatives:

> 'What are the authorities actually after? Is it a vanity, a cosmetic, exercise? Do they think we should be out of the way of the visitors? They need to do a soul-searching exercise.... To move a guy off the street into a squalid accommodation – which a lot of it is – without adequate income is not really beneficial to the guy that is moving off the street.' (street user, Westminster)

However, again as with the support providers, street users were not wholly opposed to the use of enforcement. Indeed many enthusiastically advocated the use of enforcement to terminate the anti-social (and criminal) behaviours of 'bullies', 'aggressive' beggars, and 'aggressive' ('agro') street drinkers:

> '[Aggressive beggars] should be locked up. That's the way I feel, because it's intimidating to people.... They have to be taught they can't do it.' (street user, Westminster)

Furthermore, some street users who had been imprisoned (see Chapter 4, especially the section on ASBOs) acknowledged that enforcement had been effective at terminating their participation in activities that were having a negative effect on the public:

'I was upset every time 'cos it did seem like they were picking on me quite a bit. But now looking back I can see that they [the police] were doing their job, you know. I was being a public nuisance and they, they were there to stop me from being a public nuisance.... It did seem like victimisation but we deserved it at the end of the day.' (street user, Brighton)

Where individuals are participating in street activities without presenting any such tangible threat to anyone else, however, street users on the whole believed that they should be 'left alone':

'Tell them [the police] to pick on the pillocks that mug old ladies. Leave us alone, we're not doing any harm.' (street user, Brighton)

Thus, the vast majority of street users believed that people should have the right to beg as long as they adhered to a widely accepted 'begging etiquette', comprising the precepts that people who beg should: (a) always be polite (even if members of public are rude or abusive); (b) never persist if someone has refused to give money; (c) never follow anyone; and (d) express gratitude for 'drops' regardless of the amount given. There were, however, differences of opinion with regards to begging beside ATM machines and 'spot' begging: some street users regarded these approaches to be 'permissible' (as long as the etiquette described above is adhered to), while others felt that such practices could be intimidating for some members of public.

In a similar way, street users generally argued that individuals should have the right to drink outdoors in public spaces so long as they were not engaging in ASB by shouting or swearing at the public, or being overly loud and/or generally 'obnoxious'. They therefore resented the fact that many forms of enforcement (particularly the 'softer' ones) did not seem to differentiate between 'anti-social' street users and others, but rather "label us all with that anti-social stigma" (street user, Westminster). These perceptions serve to strengthen the resolve of many street users to fight 'the system' by resisting offers of support and continuing in a street lifestyle:

'Personally it [enforcement] strengthens my resolve to stay where I am.' (street user, Westminster)

Such resolve was often heightened by poor relationships with mainstream 'beat' police officers and, especially, police community support officers (PCSOs), whom street users felt often dealt with them in a patronising or provocative manner, all too often evoking an aggressive response:

Street user 1: 'I was begging down x street one day and two coppers came up to me and one said (excuse my language, yeah?) "Move now or you're fucking nicked" ... So I told him to fuck off.'
Street user 2 [interrupts]: 'Yeah, we should be talking about aggressive coppers and non-aggressive coppers, not beggars!'
Street user 1: 'So he ... asked why I had jigged him up like that. And I said "Well, basically, you didn't respect me.... You came at me with attitude, so I gave you attitude back."' (street user focus group, Southwark)

In sharp contrast, both street users and support providers highlighted the benefits of dedicated street community policing teams, who typically take time to talk to street users and have a greater understanding of the challenges they face. This meant that they were often recognised as having a genuine concern for the well-being of vulnerable street users, who in turn were more likely to report incidents of bullying and violence on the streets:

'If you need 'owt, they're there to help you.... The homeless police are very good, I must admit.... They check on people that's sleeping in doorways and that and they make sure that they're alright. And if like, there's been a, a ruck with a homeless person they sort it out.' (street user, Westminster)

As with support providers, street user accounts indicated that enforcement interventions often led not only to geographical displacement of street activity, but also diversion into acquisitive crime (these issues are discussed in more detail in Chapter 4):

'It doesn't cure anything, it just moves you to somewhere else.... I just moved out of that zone.' (street user, Southwark)

'It pushed me to do a little bit of shoplifting, petty shoplifting, which I wasn't happy about, but I had no choice.' (street user, Leeds)

Linked to this, and again like most (homelessness) support providers, street users were generally pessimistic about the long-term outcomes of coercive drug or alcohol treatment. They argued that personal 'crises', such as a marked decline in physical health or the death of a drug-using peer, were much more likely to motivate them to address their addiction than external pressures toward treatment (see also Marlowe, 2001):

'You've got to do it for yourself. If you're forced into it it's just going to be a waste of money and they're wasting the person's time really to be honest. In my experience people that have been pushed into it, or myself who's been pushed into it, never done it, never ever succeeded.' (street user, Leeds)

Against this, we also encountered a range of instances where use of enforcement – particularly in its 'harder' forms, such as ASBOs – was acknowledged by street users as having benefited them. The circumstances in which this occurred are explored in Chapters 4 and 5.

ADAM

Aged 33, Adam was living in shared accommodation run by a drug treatment agency while subject to a two-year ASBO for begging. He had lived in local authority care from the age of 12, where he was introduced to drugs by other residents in a children's home. Adam claimed that much of his life could be described as "a mission to self-destruct", evidenced by a self-perpetuating cycle of drug abuse, dealing, burglary, prison and homelessness (including extended periods of rough sleeping): "I'd lost interest in life really, I didn't want to know.... It was get up in the morning, do what I had to do and spend the rest of the day using drugs". He was targeted by a street community police team and arrested regularly for begging, while being offered intensive support by the street outreach team. Having lost hope of ever being drug free because of previous relapses, Adam rejected all supportive interventions at the time. He was served an ASBO but carried on begging and breached it several times: "I didn't care what they were saying.... If you want to send me to prison, send me to prison". Adam had recently served a 10-week sentence for breaching his ASBO and had successfully remained 'clean' since release, but found it difficult to explain why treatment had 'worked' this time. His health had improved dramatically, he had re-entered education, was working as a volunteer, and looked forward to establishing a relationship with a daughter he had never met. He concluded that "I think I am probably an ASBO success story.... I had my first clean birthday as an adult about two weeks ago".

Conclusions

This chapter has reviewed the perspectives of the wider community, enforcement agents, support providers and street users on the justice and effectiveness of enforcement approaches. All research participants agreed that both protecting the public from ASB by street users (albeit employing differing definitions of ASB) *and* promoting the well-being of street users were important considerations, but the degree of emphasis on these two elements differed markedly between the various groups interviewed.

Enforcement agent and wider community representatives clearly considered enforcement strategies to have been 'successful' if they reduced the visibility of, and public concern about, street activities in the targeted localities. Concerns about the well-being of street users and potential displacement were highlighted, but as secondary considerations. Judged from this perspective, the enforcement programmes employed in the case study areas were considered to have been extremely successful.

As one might expect, support providers and street users placed far greater emphasis on the impact of enforcement on the well-being of those targeted by enforcement measures. This led to a more complex and ambivalent set of views regarding the effectiveness and justice of the enforcement agenda. Many support providers and frontline workers, as well as some street users, acknowledged that enforcement could play a valuable role as a 'lever', pushing street users to engage with services and make positive changes in their lives. While acknowledging that there was a need to protect the community from the consequences of anti-social street activity, support providers in particular considered enforcement to have been effective only if it had motivated street users to engage with (appropriate and accessible) services and to discontinue behaviours that were damaging to themselves as well as to the wider community. At the same time, concerns focused on:

- disproportionate and discretionary forms of enforcement;
- geographical displacement of street users and activities;
- diversion (from begging) into potentially more damaging activities, such as shoplifting and sex work;
- the long-term effectiveness of enforced drug and alcohol treatment;
- (for support providers) the strategic impacts on homelessness support providers, and in particular their relationship with clients and with local authorities.

The next chapter evaluates the merits and demerits of specific types of enforcement measures.

4

Merits and demerits of specific enforcement measures

Introduction

This chapter examines in detail each form of enforcement action used within the case studies, taking into account the perspective of all relevant stakeholders. It begins by examining what might be termed the 'harder' forms of enforcement (including ASBOs, injunctions and arrests), before moving on to analyse the 'softer' interventions employed (such as controlled drinking zones, Dispersal Orders and designing out) (see the descriptions of each in Chapter 1). As noted in Chapter 1, this broad structure is not intended to suggest that these interventions can be arranged along a strict continuum of severity.

ASBOs

It is important to commence this section by highlighting the gulf between rhetoric and reality regarding the use of ASBOs to address 'problem street culture' in the case study areas, in that far fewer street users had been issued with these orders than was commonly assumed (see Chapter 2 for the relevant statistics on each case study area):

'There's been a lot more talk about enforcement and ASBOs and everything than has actually happened on the ground.' (frontline worker, Westminster)

Street users were also subject to seriously misleading 'ASBO mythology' founded on inaccurate understandings of ASBO legislation and implementation. For example:

'If you get ASBO'd three times [breach three times] you automatically get sectioned.' (street user, Southwark)

Notwithstanding such misconceptions about the nature of ASBOs and the scale of their use, there is no doubt that these orders were a crucial ingredient in strategies to address begging and street drinking:

'Apart from one person, every ASBO that we've had for begging has been one hundred per cent successful i.e. they do not come back into this area, they don't beg. It's ridiculously successful as far as begging is concerned.' (police representative, Birmingham)

The key benefit of ASBOs, from the perspective of enforcement authorities, has been that they provide the means to impose longer custodial sentences for persistent engagement in street activity than did the relevant criminal law (see below):[4]

'The reason for putting an ASBO in for begging or being persistently drunk and disorderly is to increase the penalties at court. It takes into account the cumulative effect of someone's offending.' (police representative, Southwark)

Records in each case study area indicated that almost all street users served with ASBOs had breached the specified conditions at least once (often many times), and several had served prison sentences of up to two years as a consequence. However, this should not be interpreted as proof that ASBOs 'do not work' in reducing ASB (as is often implied in the media) in the long term. On the contrary, there was consistent evidence from across the case studies that, while almost all street users 'tested the water' when first served with an ASBO, this decreased over time as they took the Orders more seriously:

'Initially people tried it on and they thought "Ah well, nothing's gonna happen", but it became quite obvious quite soon that they were being arrested on a daily basis whenever they breached it, and they started getting some nasty sentences at court as well.' (police representative, Birmingham)

Moreover, it was clear that even the threat of an ASBO could have a powerful deterrent effect, with many street users discontinuing street activity at each stage during structured processes of escalating enforcement. For example, of the 20 street drinkers in Camberwell given an ABC, only six progressed to a full ASBO, and many other members of the street drinking school (who were not given ABCs) also moderated their behaviour and spent shorter periods drinking in groups outdoors (see Chapter 2).

More generally, ASBOs were thought not only to act as a powerful disincentive for ASB for those directly targeted, they were also thought to have an indirect deterrent effect on others involved in street activities in the area:

'The ASBO is what scares people because that's the thing that's really gonna impact on their life.' (police representative, Birmingham)

Given the 'power' of this intervention, and the vulnerability of some of the street users on whom it was targeted, it was unsurprising to find some support providers who were vehemently opposed to all use of ASBOs. These support providers were, almost without exception, working in areas where the ASBOs served were often constructed poorly and did not involve any input from support agencies. On balance, however, most support providers felt that the use of ASBOs with street users was legitimate, as a last resort, when all offers of (appropriate and accessible) supportive interventions had been refused and all attempts at getting a street user to desist from street activity had failed. Most support

---

[4] However, it should be noted that *R v Kirby [2005] EWCA Crim 1228* held that ASBOs should not normally be granted where the underlying objective was to give the court higher sentencing powers than would be permitted under ordinary criminal law. Also, *R v Boness & 10 ORS [2005] EWCA Crim 2395* held that the court should not impose an ASBO that prohibited an offender from a specified criminal act if the sentence that could be passed following conviction for the relevant offence would be a sufficient deterrent. This suggests that serious criminal offences should not be included in ASBO prohibitions but minor criminal offences, such as begging, can be included because the penalties under criminal law may be considered an inadequate deterrent for persistent offenders.

providers also insisted that, for ASBOs to be legitimate, those targeted had to pose a 'genuine' threat to other people. This accorded with street user views, as noted in Chapter 3, in that they too agreed that 'harder' forms of enforcement such as ASBOs are justified with people who beg aggressively and street drinkers who abuse or threaten other people.

Moreover, we obtained direct evidence, across all the case studies, of ASBOs having had a positive impact on the lives of some of the street users targeted themselves, especially where they were accompanied by intensive support packages. For example:

> 'As I say this ASBO, in a kind of weird way, has done me a favour because I've faced my demons ... I've chilled out, I've slowed down, you know what I mean.' (street user, Southwark)

While it is too early to determine how sustained these positive outcomes of ASBOs will be for such individuals, a number of them were now optimistic about the future, with one going as far as to suggest that his ASBO may have saved his life:

> Street user: 'I'm eating three meals a day, I'm, I'm feeling, you know, positive.... I want to change my criminality, I want to change who I am and who, and who I've become, you know. I want a better life for myself really and that's why I'm here [rehabilitation centre] because there comes a time where you just get sick of it....'
> Interviewer: 'Where would you be now do you think if you hadn't had your ASBO?'
> Street user: 'Dead or in jail on a life sentence or something.' (street user, Brighton)

On the other hand, and again across all of our case studies, we encountered individuals for whom being served with an ASBO had had a serious negative effect, typically by 'forcing' them (in their view) to continue participating in street activities in a more covert manner and/or 'driving' them into acquisitive crime in order to maintain an ongoing drug habit.

> '[The ASBO] really, really gets me because now I mean ... what do I do? Do I go out asking for a bit of change and risk getting nicked for that or should I just go out and burgle somebody's house? I'm going to get the same amount of prison time so what difference does it make?... Like I shouldn't be using drugs, yeah, right, I shouldn't be but I am, yeah, and I'm trying to use them as legal as possible, do you know what I mean? So what they're doing is just not on, not really. It upsets me it really does.' (street user, Brighton)

One young man was extremely bitter about being forced (as he perceived it) into street sex work as a direct result of receiving a begging-related ASBO that barred him from the city centre:

> 'Anti-social behaviours slapped on me ... I can't sell the *Issue*, can't beg and survive like I did, 'cause I'm not allowed in the ... city. Now because of them orders I am into the business with the passing walking trade of professional punters, and getting it off in their offices and cars, but who cares so long as they pay.' (street user, Birmingham)

Others, while admitting that they had 'improved' their behaviour as a result of an ASBO, were highly resistant to any notion that it had had a profound (positive) impact on them:

> 'It ain't changed me. It's changed my behaviour because I've had to change unless I like jail.... It ain't changed me as a person.' (street user, Birmingham)

It should be noted, however, that we encountered no evidence of ASBOs being considered 'badges of honour' among street users, as has been reported in relation to some young people, for example.

The range of factors that appeared to underpin street users' divergent attitudes and responses to ASBOs – and other forms of enforcement – are discussed in greater detail in Chapter 5.

Prior to this, we highlight below the range of issues with ASBOs that provoked anxiety among support providers, upset or frustrated street users, and, in many instances, also worried enforcement agents themselves. It should be noted that some of the criticisms summarised below relate to early 'mistakes' with the first ASBOs served to street users (many of which were particularly poorly designed and implemented), and from which 'lessons have been learned', as described below.[5]

Disproportionate penalties: support providers commonly expressed concern regarding what they viewed as disproportionate penalties for breach of an ASBO, particularly when these orders were related to 'victimless' offences such as begging:

> 'I mean that's the whole issue with this imprisonment as well; it's disproportionate. I mean people mug people at knifepoint and they get treated far more leniently.... I don't have a problem with the ABC/ASBO process, it's what it leads to that really causes problems. And when you just compare that with tariffs for violent crime and other things, it's just impossible to justify.' (support provider, Southwark)

Application process 'weighted against' vulnerable individuals: some support providers see ASBOs as overly harsh interventions, weighted against vulnerable individuals, some of whom do not have the ability and support networks necessary to 'defend' themselves. This is particularly true of individuals who have mental health problems or suffer from impaired cognitive function as a result of conditions such as Korsakoff's syndrome (sometimes referred to as 'alcoholic dementia') (see Chapter 5).

Geographical exclusions and displacement: as noted in Chapter 3, enforcement action as a whole was often criticised for causing geographical displacement of street activities, with a number of attendant problems for both the destination community and the street users themselves, who may become distanced from support services and networks. Thus, the tendency of some authorities to push for wide geographical exclusions when applying for ASBOs came under fire from a range of informants:

> 'One lesson we have learned is that geographical exclusion isn't necessarily a good thing. There's a real tendency for authorities who are ASBO-ing people and excluding them geographically from other boroughs to pass the problems on to other people.' (local authority representative, Southwark)

This said, most interviewees accepted that it may sometimes be necessary to offer particular communities plagued by anti-social street culture some respite by banning street users from carefully defined areas. Some support providers also argued that street users

---

5   Thus, in *R v Boness & 10 ORS [2005] EWCA Crim 2395*, it was held that (post-conviction) ASBOs had to be tailor-made for the individual offender, proportionate and commensurate with the risk guarded against, and should not be drafted too widely or with insufficient clarity.

themselves may benefit from being banned from city centres because that is where they are most likely to make the "fast buck" needed to feed their damaging addictions – as "there are always new faces to blag in the city centre" (support provider, Birmingham).

Inappropriate behavioural conditions: while behavioural conditions were generally viewed as a more effective mechanism for prompting positive lifestyle changes among street users than geographical exclusions, criticism regarding some of the specific conditions attached to ASBOs served to street users was widespread:

> 'The difficulty that we have with ASBOs, certainly post-conviction ASBOs that've been issued elsewhere … [is] they've been served on very vulnerable individuals, they've come from out of nowhere, they've put a whole host of very silly conditions on the order and because they haven't been contested, because the individual has probably only had the services of the duty solicitor on the day, is that these ASBOs have got through with all these really silly prohibitions on them.' (police representative, Southwark)

Criticisms of ASBO behavioural conditions were typically founded on some combination of the following concerns:

- Unrealistic or excessively wide prohibitions: particularly in the early days of ASBO implementation, behavioural conditions could be so restrictive as to severely impinge on vulnerable street users' quality of life. Moreover, some ASBO conditions made it virtually impossible for someone with an addiction to avoid breaching them, even if they were making a concerted effort to discontinue involvement in street activities. For example, a street drinker in one case study area was banned from entering any on- or off-licence premises in the whole region, and a magistrate interviewed had encountered an ASBO banning an alcoholic from drinking "alcoholic liquor either inside or outside anywhere. So, teetotal.... No chance, is there?".
- Inclusion of (unrelated) criminal offences: the inclusion of prohibitions on serious (and unrelated) criminal activities – such as assault or burglary – within ASBOs targeted on street drinking or begging aroused particular concern. As these activities are already subject to (severe) penalties under the criminal law, this was viewed as giving enforcement agencies an unjustified 'two cracks at the whip'. There were especially strong objections to the inclusion of such conditions when they were motivated by an offence committed many years ago and punishment for the original offence had already been served.[6]
- Inclusion of 'innocent' everyday activities: ASBO conditions often targeted the "precursory acts" to criminal or anti-social behaviours so that, for example, a drug user might be prohibited from having foil on their person. While such conditions could be justified as 'preventative' measures, they clearly leave open the possibility of abuse. There is the potential, for example, for a person subject to some such condition to be imprisoned for up to five years for as innocent an act as having a foil covered biscuit in their pocket ('the kitkat phenomenon'). While it was accepted that in practice such gross abuse of ASBO legislation is unlikely to be permitted by magistrates, many support providers (and some enforcement agents) felt that it was inappropriate for the law to be framed in such a way to allow even this theoretical possibility.

Inconsistency of implementation: major inconsistencies were reported in magistrates' attitudes toward the 'seriousness' of street activity; their consequent receptiveness to ASBO

---

[6] See footnote 4, on page 30.

applications; and in the penalties imposed for breach. In particular, support providers and enforcement agents alike often commented on the inconsistent definitions of 'passive' and 'aggressive' begging, and what constituted appropriate evidence of the harassment, alarm or distress necessary for an ABSO application to succeed. For example, while some magistrates accepted the findings of research surveys demonstrating the public's general antipathy towards people who beg as sufficient grounds to grant an ASBO for begging, one magistrate explained why he took a different view:

> 'And they came to the court … and said '"Right, now, we'd like an ASBO because he's persistent, here's his record, and we have done a survey of x residents", I can't remember what the figures were but 75% of them don't like beggars. I was rather surprised, what about the other 25%, you know? But I said "That doesn't get me or you over the hurdle that you have to establish that this particular incident which warrants this application is likely to cause harassment, alarm and distress." And they said "Well, there's the evidence, here's the survey, people don't like beggars." And I'm afraid I said "No, that's not good enough."'

Support providers, councils and police alike had come to 'expect the unexpected' with regards to the sentences imposed for breach. For example, a street user in one case study area had breached his ASBO 10 times and was sentenced to two years in prison: but on previous occasions when convicted for breach he had never faced more than a £25 fine or one night in jail. In contrast, another street user had been sentenced to six months in prison after just one breach in the same borough. Similarly, in another context it was noted that:

> 'It really does depend which judge you get on which day. It really does send out inconsistent messages to our service users, to the people on the street.' (support provider, Brighton)

Absence of 'warning' stages: two case study areas (Leeds and Birmingham) did not use ABCs, ABAs or any equivalent formalised 'warning' measure before pursuing ASBO applications with street users. However, the incorporation of such measures at an early stage along 'the ASBO route' was heralded as good practice in all of the other areas, and ABCs in particular appear to have been an effective deterrent for many street users, often quite unexpectedly (see above).

Some enforcement agents and support providers also felt that ABCs provided street users with a legitimate 'excuse' to discontinue participation in damaging street activities without 'losing face' within the street community. Moreover, they created opportunities for support workers to challenge street users and force them to acknowledge the impact that their activities were having on the broader community:

> 'It was sitting down and explaining to them their behaviour in the context of the community. It's not like "You've got a criminal record, you're bad", it's saying "Your behaviour pisses off the rest of the community."' (local authority representative, Camden)

Lack of 'room for failure': it is widely accepted that addiction is by its very nature a chronic condition, wherein progress toward abstention is often haphazard and the likelihood of relapse great (Carver, 2004; West, 2006). However, once served, ASBOs allow little room for failure. Attached prohibitions often disallow the carrying of drugs paraphernalia or consumption of alcohol in a public place, for example, thus relapse carries with it a pronounced danger of breach and (potentially) lengthy periods of incarceration. In such instances, street users may be punished (severely) for succumbing to what is an accepted stage in the process of addiction recovery.

Potential of imprisonment for breach of interim ASBOs: many (stand-alone) ASBOs were first served as interim ASBOs, on the grounds that immediate action was needed to protect the community from recipients' ASB. As noted in Chapter 1, breach of interim ASBOs is a criminal offence punishable by imprisonment, even if the main ASBO is not eventually granted at the full hearing. Although this had not occurred in any of our case studies, several interviewees expressed anxiety at the possibility of street users serving prison sentences in circumstances where a court had yet to consider the full evidence to justify an ASBO.

Reliability of hearsay evidence: support providers frequently questioned the reliability of hearsay evidence collated to support ASBO applications, given the significant risk for mistaken identity (as evidenced by the fact that ASBO papers were served to the wrong street drinker in one case study area), and the temptation its admissibility may pose to communities desperate to rid their neighbourhoods of ASB. However, a magistrate interviewed did not share these concerns:

> 'We now accept it in all sorts of different forms, hearsay evidence.... I think it's all right, you just have to be careful.'

Naming and shaming: the authorities in all but one of our case study areas elected not to publicise the identities of street users who had received ASBOs, for fear that doing so might further stigmatise them and/or even potentially induce public vigilantism. In Leeds, however, the practice of publicising the names, photographs, offences and prohibitions of street users with ASBOs was justified on the grounds that this was in line with central government guidance (see Home Office, 2003). Some business proprietors had posted these leaflets in their shop windows (despite being asked by the council not to do so). Support providers in the area argued that naming and shaming in this way 'doubly criminalises' street users, who not only have to deal with the legal penalties for street activity, but are also exposed to public vilification.

Re-criminalisation: finally, some interviewees were concerned that ASBOs did, in effect, 're-criminalise' vulnerable street users – street drinkers in particular – for whom criminal activity (such as theft or criminal damage) was a thing of the past:

> '[Most] have criminal records, but their offending history has really tailed off prior to this happening. It's almost like some of them are incapable of committing crimes. They've got lots of previous convictions for shoplifting, for deception, burglary, all sorts of things. It just stops and it's as much as they can do to go to [treatment service], get their methadone script and sit on a corner and drink a can of beer.... And that's why I was always concerned that we're basically re-criminalising these individuals.' (police representative, Southwark)

To summarise, ASBOs were a very powerful tool in strategies to address street activity, and there was broad support for use of them in tightly defined circumstances, but there were a wide range of concerns to be addressed from the perspective of both support providers and street users.

Injunctions

Alongside ASBOs, injunctions are at the 'hardest' end of enforcement because of the possibility of prison sentences for breach. However, they were not widely used within any of the case study areas to address street-related activities (none of our in-depth interviewees had received one), and were generally considered a less 'efficient' means of achieving enforcement aims than ASBOs. A key advantage of ASBOs over injunctions, from the perspective of enforcement agents, is that the consequences of breach are more serious. However, some local authorities indicated that they might seek to employ civil injunctions in the future, especially with regards to persistent passive begging, if they were struggling to convince magistrates of the harassment, alarm or distress required to serve an ASBO.

Arrests for begging

The extent to which the 1824 Vagrancy Act was used to arrest those begging seemed to depend almost entirely on the scale of begging in an area, and the consequent priority accorded to it by senior police officers. Specialist street community policing teams excepted, frontline police officers were often reluctant to arrest people for begging, regarding the procedure to be a 'waste of time'. Many frontline officers preferred simply to move them on:

> 'Core cops doing shifts and dealing with every other bit of policing perceive begging and street drinking as so minor that they don't want to trouble themselves with it.' (police representative, Westminster)

On its own, the practice of arresting people who beg was viewed as ineffective, as evidenced by high levels of repeat offending and problems with the displacement of begging activity. Eighteen of the people arrested for begging in Westminster, for example, had been arrested a sum total of 299 times between April 2003 and March 2004. In Leeds also, earlier attempts to address begging through arrests in the city centre had simply moved the problem to the university campus area.

Arresting people who beg seemed to fail to deter them for two main reasons. First, many street users 'chose' to beg on the grounds that, of the options available to them for funding an addiction (most commonly identified as begging or stealing), begging was "the least horrible on society" (street user, Southwark). Second, those begging are often unfazed by the prospect of spending a night in the cells, particularly if they are street homeless, with some regarding the risk of arrest as simply an 'occupational hazard': "You think, well I'm homeless anyway, so what have you got to lose?" (street user, Westminster).

Notably, the reclassification of begging as a 'recordable' offence (see Chapter 1), of itself, appeared to provide no additional deterrent for street users to beg (although it has been important in facilitating the job of the police in assembling evidence for post-conviction ASBOs).

All this said, a small number of street users did cite multiple arrests ("sick of being arrested") as a motivating factor for change, and some police officers argued that repeatedly arresting people, even if the outcome is only a few hours in jail each time, could be an effective tool in addressing street culture:

> 'When you arrest somebody ... being in custody means that they don't have their fix and it means that they don't feel as happy because they start to feel the

withdrawing. And that's what encourages them, in my experience and having spoken with some of the agencies, to get back in contact.' (police representative, Birmingham)

There was a virtually universal acceptance that clampdowns on 'sit-down' begging (via repeated arrests) almost inevitably led to an increase in 'spot' or 'mobile' begging – a practice widely acknowledged to be more intimidating for members of the public.

In addition, many street users admitted that they would steal rather than beg during these targeted operations if they could see no (immediate) alternative means of avoiding 'the rattle', that is, of financing their addiction and thereby averting the (potentially severe) pain of withdrawal:[7]

> Interviewer: 'What happens when the police clamp down on begging, by....'
> Street user 1 [interrupting]: 'You end up shoplifting....'
> Various: 'Yeah, yeah.'
> Street user 2: 'It's a fact.'
> Street user 3: 'If you're being threatened with jail for begging and you know you can't, you can't beg....'
> Street user 4 [interrupting]: 'You've got to earn regardless.'
> Street user 3: '... so you go out shoplifting.'
> Street user 4: 'If you've got an addiction where you have to find £30 a day, yeah, and you can't go begging....'
> Street user 5: '... 'cause you'll get arrested....'
> Street user 4: '... then you have to steal.'
> Street user 5: 'It's true.' (street user focus group, Southwark)

Finally, there was widespread consensus among frontline police officers and street users alike that fining people involved in begging was an illogical and counterproductive intervention:

> 'Well you just beg the money to pay the fine.... So they're fining you for doing something and then you have to go out and do it some more to pay the fine. So it doesn't really make an awful lot of sense.' (street user, Westminster)

ANDREW

A 33-year-old *Big Issue* vendor, Andrew was staying with friends in an attempt to avoid further arrests for sleeping rough. He had become homeless and turned to drugs "'cause it took away all my trouble" after a traumatic relationship breakdown, and had subsequently been arrested (and fined) for sleeping rough on several occasions. He had also been arrested for begging many times, but "it didn't stop me doing it because I knew I still had to beg for the drug money". While Andrew acknowledged that his life was more stable and his health much better once he was no longer

---

[7] Some existing reports suggest that anti-begging operations do not lead to an increase in acquisitive crime (see, for example, Camden Marketing, 2004), but fail to provide substantive evidence of the data underpinning such an assertion. In any case we would suggest that official crime statistics are too 'blunt' a tool to provide robust evidence on the extent of diversion into other criminal activities when street users are prevented from begging, not least because of the well-known general problems with such statistics, such as the vagaries of recording and reporting practices, and the extent to which arrest figures (and displacement of crime) are influenced by the intensity of policing in targeted localities (Maguire, 2002; Bowers and Johnson, 2003). Much more convincing, we would suggest, is the consistent and detailed qualitative evidence that we obtained from across all of the case studies that street users do shift to shoplifting during begging clampdowns.

sleeping on the street, he doubted that his strategy to avoid arrest would do him much good in the long term: "it's hard to get people who actually want to put you up, 'specially if you're a drug user ... the only people I could get to put me up were drug users which doesn't exactly help". He had been banned from several hostels for using drugs on the premises, so saw no other alternative in the short term.

Arrests for sleeping rough

Of our case study areas, only Leeds employed Section 4 of the 1824 Vagrancy Act to arrest people for sleeping rough. The others had elected not to do so, often because of objections in principle, but also in some cases because they feared a public backlash, or potential legal difficulties.

In Leeds, however, the power to arrest rough sleepers under this legislation was regarded as a powerful additional tool to disrupt street lifestyles and address associated ASB. Rough sleepers were not arrested the first time they were encountered by police, but were given a warning and a letter informing of them of local housing and support resources. If an individual was arrested for sleeping rough at a later date, the council would state in court that emergency accommodation was available for homeless people. However, both rough sleepers and frontline workers cited many instances of failing to access such accommodation due to the unavailability of bedspaces; also, many of those sleeping rough had been barred from all the hostels in the city.

Nevertheless, evidence from Leeds suggests that this particular enforcement measure can act as a constructive 'kick', motivating a minority of rough sleepers to seek accommodation:

'I think it made me realise that I had to get out of ... that little rut because when you're on the street you're as low as it can be and you're basically giving up. So because I wanted to get away from getting arrested and that I've actually started to get a bit of an act together. When I was sleeping rough, it was just the same procedure. Wake up, make money, buy drugs, go to sleep, wake up, make money, buy drugs. At least now I've started eating and that again.... I wasn't when I was sleeping rough.' (street user, Leeds)

More commonly, however, rough sleepers simply avoided arrest by bedding down in more hidden places further from the city centre:

'When I found out about them ... arresting people for sort of like vagrancy or whatever I learnt to sleep as far out of the city centre as possible.... Some of the places I've slept in were terrible, you know what I mean. But at least I knew the police wouldn't come and you wouldn't get arrested.... I slept under bridges and all sorts.' (street user, Leeds)

As with arrests for begging (see above), the practice of fining individuals for sleeping rough was viewed by support providers and street users as entirely counterproductive.

While acknowledging that the practice of sleeping rough is dangerous and exacerbates 'chaotic' drug-fuelled lifestyles, most support providers were opposed to the arrest of rough sleepers on the grounds that it did little to either motivate, or practically enable, those affected to access appropriate accommodation. Likewise, arresting rough sleepers was subject to virtually unanimous disapprobation by the members of the wider community interviewed:

'My personal view is that at the end of the day if they are genuine homeless people then they need somewhere to put their head down.' (business proprietor, Leeds)

Controlled drinking zones

Controlled drinking zones (byelaws or DPPOs) are widely used measures that are relatively simple to implement. They provide an almost instantaneous reduction in the visibility of street drinking because street users can be required by the police to stop drinking in defined areas or face having their alcohol confiscated. The policing of these interventions very rarely led to the arrest of street users (as they usually complied with police requests to stop drinking and/or to hand over their alcohol). Thus, they neither criminalised street drinkers nor consumed large amounts of police time to enforce.

However, while controlled drinking zones were highly effective at deterring street drinkers from congregating in large groups in defined areas, they did little to reduce either the need for, or inclination of, street users to drink in public spaces. Rather, these enforcement interventions largely diluted and displaced the problem, with street drinkers typically moving elsewhere to avoid having their alcohol confiscated and/or consuming it more covertly (for example, pouring alcohol into soft drink bottles or transporting cans in carrier bags).

'It's not changed my attitude at all. I still drink on the streets and will continue to drink on the streets. Well the only difference it made is I now do it more subtly.' (street user, Westminster)

'What the DPPO does is it moves it, it moves the problem…. The DPPO in and of itself doesn't solve the problem, it solves the problem *in that area*…. The DPPO plays a role as a deterrent, but I don't think it solves anything for individuals. It's the network of services that does that.' (local authority representative, Leeds)

In some ways, these interventions could be counterproductive:

Street user 1: 'You drink more because you don't know when it's next gonna be taken off you.'
Street user 2: 'It makes me upset, it makes me a lot harder against it….'
Street user 3: 'It makes us go out and get more drink.'
Street user 1: 'Actually, it makes us all shoplift, to be honest.'
Street user 3: 'Yeah, because we just spent our last tenner on beer. They took it away so we're completely skint, so the next thing we've got to do, we still want to drink, so we think "Right, where's the next drink coming from?"' (street user focus group, Brighton)

Street drinkers felt acutely discriminated against given the discretionary policing of controlled drinking zones. In their view this practice renders 'poor drinking' (by street drinkers outdoors) to be unacceptable, when other 'wealthy' members of the public can engage in the very same activity without fear of reprisal.

Street users were also enraged by the idea of their property being destroyed, with one drawing a parallel with inappropriate use of stereo equipment in public places:

'I don't think they've actually got any right to do that [confiscate alcohol] because you paid for that. Say if you had something expensive on you and they took that off you and smashed it on the floor. They'd [only] say "You're not listening to that because you're causing a nuisance to the public".... I think the principle's wrong, it's unfair, they shouldn't throw the drink away.' (street user, Birmingham)

The consequent anger among those affected, and tendency for street drinkers to become fixated on the 'injustice' of 'de-canning' – particularly when the cans/bottles are unopened – can act as a barrier to effective supportive interventions. As one frontline worker explained:

'Once the messages get blurred – it's unacceptable for you to drink, but it's fine for those two stockbrokers over there to drink – when that happens I completely lose the moral high ground I might have in terms of applying enforcement and complying with social rules agenda. The conversation becomes one of "You're picking on me".... I've lost that tool, which had been an incredibly valuable one.' (support provider, Westminster)

Perhaps most fundamentally, controlled drinking zones neither provide alternatives to, nor challenge the 'logic' of, drinking on the street for long-term street drinkers. These individuals drink outdoors for a number of reasons, including the following: they want to socialise but cannot afford to drink in a pub; they are not permitted to have visitors and/ or alcohol in most hostels; or, for those with accommodation, they are reluctant to invite fellow drinkers back to their own home for fear that their behaviour may jeopardise the security of their tenancy. One support provider explained this dilemma as follows:

'I always maintained you could clear Camberwell Green in five minutes with Wetherspoons vouchers.... People don't want to be there. They're just there because it's the least worst option.' (support provider, Southwark)

SAM

Aged 47, Sam had been homeless for slightly more than one year and was living in a rolling shelter at the time of interview. Previously, he had begun drinking heavily when his business went downhill, got into rent arrears, was eventually evicted, and ended up sleeping rough. Sam had had alcohol confiscated on several occasions when drinking outdoors within a DPPO since becoming homeless. He argued that the enforcement of controlled drinking zones was appropriate "if you've got people that are completely out of their faces", but that casual moderate drinking on the street of the kind he engaged in "is not harmful to anybody" and should be permitted. Given his experience of being 'de-canned' when other people were allowed to consume vast quantities of alcohol outside bars nearby, Sam was very resentful of the implication that "you're not allowed to drink on the streets of x unless you're in a suit ... it's unfair". Sam still drank in public places despite the imposition of the DPPO, but he was careful about camouflaging his alcohol: "I used to drink out of a can.... I've now disguised it". He had no intention of reducing his alcohol intake in the near future – attributing his consumption largely to boredom – but was working as a *Big Issue* vendor and planned to re-enter the mainstream workforce and "get back on track" once he had secured more permanent accommodation.

Dispersal Orders

Dispersal Orders had been on the agenda as a potential tool to combat anti-social street culture in a few of the case study areas, but they had not been utilised to any great extent (see Chapter 2). While a Dispersal Order could in theory have the benefit of breaking up large groups of street users, they raised the usual concerns about displacement:

> 'You only move things on, you know, they only shift to another area and it's still going to happen…. You can't deal with it like that, you can only move people around. The people are still there … they'll just be even more subversive and harder to find, you know. They'll hide better, you'll drive them further underground.' (street user, Southwark)

Rough sleeping hotspot closure

The coordinated closure of rough sleeping hotspots – utilised most commonly in central London but also in Birmingham and elsewhere – was deemed to be an effective strategy by enforcement agents and frontline workers alike. This was because, where properly implemented, it could be used as a valuable tool with which outreach workers were able to 'lever' entrenched street users into services:

> 'If an area is disrupted then it might budge someone in their pattern of going to the same place, at the same time. If they can no longer do that it may make them look at something else. That works for the odd person.' (frontline worker, Westminster)

All agencies involved in the closure of hotspots acknowledged that some displacement was inevitable, but felt that the 'net gain' generated through directing people into support services (particularly accommodation) justified the intervention.

They did emphasise, however, the need for appropriate interagency coordination, and careful phasing, such that street users were given plenty of warning regarding the date of closure and information about support options available. All were clear that eventual closure should be preceded by very intensive outreach work, including ring-fenced services to ensure that responsive individuals were integrated into services immediately.

Designing out

Adaptation of the urban environment to design out street activity, that is, to make hotspots less habitable and easier to police, has been integral to initiatives in each of the case study areas. Common environmental modifications have included the installation of lighting and CCTV, together with the removal of vegetation, seating and walls in areas previously appropriated by groups of street drinkers and rough sleepers. Local authorities sometimes encouraged public involvement in this process, providing resources for community members to replant gardens in parks previously serving as a base for street drinking, for example, so that they could participate in the proactive 'reclamation' of public space.

One case study area (Westminster) also adopted 'hot-washing' as a strategy to make certain areas inhospitable for people sleeping rough. Here, street cleaners were tasked with spraying pavements in specified areas to deter rough sleepers from bedding down. While this was justified by the local authority on the premise that it was a deterrent that may (in combination with other measures) potentially encourage rough sleepers to 'come inside', all of the rough sleepers we encountered who had been directly affected merely found alternative 'out of the way' places to sleep.

Hot-washing elicited particularly severe criticism from frontline workers:

> 'It's inhumane.... These are some of the most vulnerable people in society.... They expect to be knocked by society. It's the norm for them. But I personally think it's a pretty appalling way to treat people.' (frontline worker, Westminster)

The environmental measures described above appear to have been very effective at removing street activities from targeted areas, but it is difficult to discern any benefits for street users.

Alternative giving schemes

Alternative giving schemes seemed to be a fairly marginal element in strategies to address street culture. The sum of donations collected tended to be insignificant in most areas (see also Hermer, 1999), particularly when viewed in the context of the multi-million pound annual turnovers of some major homeless charities. Birmingham's scheme seemed to be the most successful among our case studies, raising around £20,000 in each of its three years of operation, with these monies used to pay for items (such as travel passes and birth certificates) for homeless people that are difficult to fund from other sources.

However, it can be argued that the key purpose of alternative giving schemes is not to raise funds, but rather to educate the public and to dissuade them from giving money directly to those who beg. While official evaluations report that a significant proportion of members of the public surveyed claim that they would or might stop giving as a result of such campaigns (see, for example, Camden Marketing, 2004), our interviews suggested that these had little effect on the day-to-day takings of those begging, and may in fact be counterproductive:

> 'I was begging when that [campaign] came out and I got more money. I did better, 'cos people used to say to me "I will not be told who to give money to and when I can give it". So I actually did quite well out of it. Most of the people that was begging around that time did. [The public] did not like to be treated like fools.' (street user, Westminster)

Street users were almost universally hostile to alternative giving schemes, but support providers were more ambivalent. On the one hand they were acutely aware of the potentially damaging impact that begging had on individuals' health (because of the strong positive correlation between the amount of money acquired and quantity of drugs consumed), but at the same time they feared that publicising the links between begging and drug abuse ran the risk of "turning off the public's compassion switch" (support provider, Westminster).

Regulation of *Big Issue* vendors

While the main focus of this study was on street drinking, begging and rough sleeping, in a number of case studies the enforcement agenda had also impacted on those engaged in selling the *Big Issue* street magazine. In Birmingham, for example, the number of city centre pitches had been reduced, and green tabards were introduced to denote 'genuine vendors'. Similar measures were put in place in Leeds. As these measures were designed to counter attempts to use the *Big Issue* as a front for begging, they were often strongly supported by both local vendors and *Big Issue* staff, and the resultant improved relations between 'genuine' vendors and the police were also commented on:

> 'The vendors actively report people they know are doing this "one mag blag" ... in the past, before they had the green tabards, you used to have to get on their case quite a bit because you didn't know if they were a genuine vendor until you went over and spoke to them and filled out the forms and checked them through the PNC [Police National Computer].... We have to harass the genuine vendors a lot less than we used to....' (police representative, Birmingham)

In some case studies street users who had been targeted by enforcement agents for begging had been actively encouraged to get 'badged up' to sell the *Big Issue*. On the one hand, this gave street users an opportunity to generate income 'legitimately' (legally) and provided routine to their day, but on the other hand, it increased competition for the custom of clientele at a time when the number of pitches available to vendors was being reduced in many cities. Furthermore, selling the *Big Issue* was not a 'viable' alternative to begging for street users with an expensive drug habit, given that begging tends to be far more lucrative (see also Fitzpatrick and Kennedy, 2000):

> 'You can't earn enough selling the *Big Issue*, not really [to sustain a habit]. So I didn't sell the *Big Issue*, I was just begging.' (street user, Westminster)

Conclusions

This chapter has reviewed the range of specific enforcement interventions used to tackle street culture across our case studies. A wide range of detailed points were made, but the main overall findings were as follows:

- ASBOs were by far the most powerful, and controversial, tool employed to tackle street culture. While there had been fewer ASBOs granted against street users than is commonly supposed, they clearly had had a strong (direct and indirect) deterrent effect on those engaged in street activities. While most support providers, as well as street users, thought the use of ASBOs against street users was justified in very specific circumstances, a wide range of concerns about their design and implementation in practice were voiced. We had direct evidence from across the case studies of street users for whom being 'ASBO'd' had had a profound impact on their lives – either positive or negative.
- Arresting people for begging, on its own, was viewed as largely ineffective (although there were some counterviews). There was strong evidence of a shift from sit-down to mobile begging during clampdowns, and also evidence of diversion into other forms of crime.
- Street users were only arrested for sleeping rough in one case study area; this was a practice disapproved of by the great majority of those we interviewed.
- In contrast, carefully coordinated and planned rough sleeping hotspot closure was viewed as a potentially valuable lever in moving people on from street lifestyles.
- While the softer forms of enforcement – such as controlled drinking zones and designing out – were often viewed as highly effective from the community's perspective, there was little evidence of benefits to street users.

5

When can enforcement benefit street users?

Introduction

The previous two chapters have reviewed research participants' general views of enforcement and their perceptions of specific enforcement mechanisms. We have established that, notwithstanding the wide range of concerns about the practical implementation of enforcement in many areas, most support providers and some street users, as well as virtually all enforcement agents, feel that enforcement (particularly in its harder forms) has a role to play in helping some street users as well as the wider community.

This chapter now clarifies, insofar as possible, the circumstances in which enforcement action is most likely to have positive benefits for the *street users themselves*. It begins by considering the range of ways in which street users may respond to enforcement action, as their response crucially determines whether 'positive' outcomes are likely to result. It then moves on to examine the policy and practice conditions that appear necessary for there to be any reasonable prospect of a positive outcome of enforcement for street users, and, finally, explores the personal circumstances that make such positive outcomes more or less likely to result.

Potential responses of street users to enforcement

When street users face the threat or implementation of enforcement they have a limited number of courses of action open to them, including:

- to engage with support providers and/or modify their behaviour (to lessen or discontinue the negative impact of their street activities on the wider community);
- to disregard the threat or action of enforcement and continue participating in street activities (usually in a more covert manner) with the attendant risk of (increasingly severe) punitive outcomes;
- to leave the targeted area and continue participation in a street lifestyle elsewhere ('geographical displacement');
- (in the case of begging) to adopt alternative means of funding an addiction, for example, acquisitive crime or sex work ('activity displacement').

Only where they pursue the first of these courses of action might we regard enforcement as having had a positive outcome for street users (or indeed the wider public). We should make it clear at this point that we consider even a temporary cessation of street activities to represent 'success', as this may, for example, be crucial to stabilising a vulnerable street user's health, as well as providing some respite for the wider community. While sustained lifestyle changes are clearly the optimal outcome, given the newness of the enforcement agenda it was too early to say how durable the positive outcomes identified would prove to be in the long term. However, it was clear that in a minority of the cases we encountered, the use of hard forms of enforcement – particularly ASBOs – had contributed to street users engaging with service providers in a way that they had not done hitherto.

Some of the other potential courses of action outlined above may have particularly negative effects on street users, distancing them from existing sources of support or pushing them towards even more dangerous and damaging lifestyles. Moreover, the response of street users to enforcement action is highly unpredictable. Enforcement agents, support providers and street users themselves found it difficult to account for the divergent responses, with many reporting that they had been very surprised at the outcomes for specific individuals, or, in the case of street users, their own reactions.

> 'There were people who had ASBOs who we thought were set up to fail and we were wrong because they have changed their behaviour.' (support provider, Southwark)

This is closely related to the unpredictability of responses to drug and alcohol treatment. Even those who had successfully undergone rehabilitation (often after many previous 'failed' attempts) found it difficult to understand why it had 'worked' this time, other than that they had (for whatever reason) come to a point where they were 'ready'.

> Interviewer: 'So what, what's made the difference this time around?'
> Street user: 'I really don't know…. Everyone mentions that time when they've had enough and it was just that time for me.' (street user, Brighton)

The unpredictability of street users' responses to enforcement and drug/alcohol treatment, coupled with the very real possibility of significant negative impacts for some, makes enforcement action a 'high risk' strategy with regards to the well-being of street users. But given the very desperate (indeed life-threatening) circumstances of some of the most vulnerable street users, many support providers and frontline workers took the view that the use of enforcement was a risk worth taking:

> 'I'm happy to go down the enforcement route when we've tried everything else and the person is still gradually killing themselves and we're getting nowhere…. We've seen it happen [displacement from begging into sex work], and I guess the trade-off is – what can I say – from our point of view it has been worth it. Things are better now, despite the fact of all this.' (support provider, Birmingham)

Moreover, while it is impossible to predict with certainty when enforcement will and will not lead to beneficial outcomes for specific street users, it is possible to identify: (a) *policy and practice* conditions conducive to positive outcomes; and (b) the *personal characteristics and circumstances* of street users that appear to make them more or less likely to respond in positive ways. Importantly, while the latter are largely beyond the realm of authorities' control, policy makers and practitioners do have some degree of influence over the former. These points are explored in detail below.

TIM

Aged 27 at the point of interview, Tim was undergoing residential rehabilitation after being released early on a 'tag' after spending nine months (of a two-year sentence) in prison for breaching an ASBO. He had developed psychological dependence on morphine after being injured in a serious accident as a teenager, later progressed to harder drugs (including crack cocaine), and funded his addiction via theft and drug dealing. Prior to being 'ASBO'd' his life had, in his opinion, "escalated into complete mayhem", such that after "losing the plot completely" he had slept rough, 'spot' begged and used the *Big Issue* as a tool to beg. Being "completely out of it", he consistently rejected the support services offered to him and was finally served an ASBO for aggressive begging. Tim "kind of" tried to abide by the conditions of his ASBO (which prohibited him from begging or holding any *Big Issue* magazines and banned him from a number of specified streets), but he found it difficult to do so when he was "rattling": "when you need the drugs, who cares, you know?". He therefore ended up breaching on several occasions. Tim claimed that his ASBO and consequent incarceration may potentially have saved his life given his chaotic lifestyle and poor state of health at the time, as it enabled him to get 'clean' and stay that way for a sustained period. At the time of interview he was in good health, hoped to re-enter education, and was optimistic about the future, but only cautiously so given his past history of relapse following periods of stabilisation.

JOHN

Aged 27, John had spent extensive periods of his life sleeping rough, but was living in a hostel when interviewed. He had been physically and sexually abused as a child and had used heroin to "block everything out" since the age of 17. Since then, John had been in and out of prison for shoplifting and burglary offences that he had committed to fund his addiction. He had been arrested for begging on several occasions, been given an ASBO for begging, and had served several short prison sentences for breaching his ASBO (12 months in total). He was on a methadone script, but continued to 'top up' with heroin. John aspired to reduce his drug intake but could not see himself terminating drug use completely in the foreseeable future as he claimed to "need something in me system to cope.... I'm not ready to go without anything, basically". He had been 'clean' on prison release on more than one occasion previously and "had all good intentions but as soon as I got out that gate I just couldn't help myself from wanting to score and use". He was very angry about his ASBO, claiming it forced him to beg more covertly and to steal when he would prefer to give people the option of giving to him rather than just "taking from them": "I'd still rather go out there and beg instead of going burgling somebody's house at the end of the day".

Impact of policy and practice conditions

A number of conditions within local policy and practice frameworks appear to be conducive to beneficial outcomes for street users. The existence of these conditions in no way guarantees success, but positive outcomes appear highly unlikely if these arrangements are not in place when any enforcement initiative is implemented.

Supportive interventions are integrated with enforcement action

Given the complex support needs of most street users, isolated (especially 'soft') enforcement interventions, such as controlled drinking zones and/or hot-washing, may lessen the negative impact of street activity on local communities, but they will not in and of themselves bring about positive lifestyle change for members of the street population.

It is clear that, to be effective, enforcement initiatives must be accompanied by comprehensive packages of *appropriate* and *accessible* support that can be tailored to meet individual needs – most especially drug or alcohol treatment, but also mental health services, accommodation and practical, social and emotional support. While the provision of intensive support will not guarantee a positive outcome, this support must be in place if frontline workers are to make the most of the 'window of opportunity' that enforcement may present:

> 'I personally think it's [enforcement is] making all our clients sit back and think to some level or another.... But timing is 90% of what outreach is about. It's about being there to offer things at the right moment for someone and to have everything in place to run with that person when they are motivated. The important thing is how well set up everything else is when the ASBO is given.' (frontline worker, Southwark)

A number of problems within the network of support services did, however, continue to limit the potential utility of enforcement strategies in particular localities. These included:

- difficulty in achieving diagnoses and accessing adequate treatment, including counselling, for street users with mental health problems;
- lengthy delays in accessing drug and alcohol treatment (while drug treatment services had improved significantly in some areas, this was far less true with regards to alcohol);
- the unsuitability of many existing drug and alcohol treatment programmes for vulnerable street users;
- ongoing problems with the long-term 'parking' of street users on high dosage methadone prescriptions with little support or motivation to move away from a drug-centred lifestyle in the long term;
- inadequate post-resettlement and post-treatment support contributing to high relapse rates;
- in some areas, difficulties in gaining access to both emergency and long-term accommodation.

Enforcement initiatives involve effective interagency working

Enforcement initiatives seemed much more likely to bring about positive outcomes for street users (and the wider community) where they involved effective interagency working between enforcement agents (especially the police) and support providers (particularly street outreach teams, accommodation providers and drug and alcohol treatment agencies). Effective joint working not only made support providers accountable – ensuring that they offered street users the services to which they were entitled – but also enabled the most effective use to be made of the 'window of opportunity' presented. The Target and Tasking model used in some of the case study areas (see Chapter 2), for example, provided:

> '... a way of ensuring that clients get the services that they should be getting and that they're entitled to. It pulls the services together.... When you sign somebody up to an ABA as well as saying the behaviour they shouldn't be doing, you'll tell them what they are entitled to. And you get other support providers to sign up to it. It's just linking everything together and making everyone work in partnership.' (support provider, Camden)

One particular point to emerge from the case studies was that the potential utility of prison sentences as a break from street lifestyles (see Chapter 3) was all too often lost as poor communication between prison staff and various support services meant that street users were released without suitable accommodation arranged and with little post-detoxification support in place. This made street users particularly susceptible to relapse, with a return to a street lifestyle an almost 'natural' (and some street users would argue inevitable) outcome.

Harder forms of enforcement incorporate warning stages

While the majority of case study areas employed 'warning' stages (for example, ABCs, ABAs or ASB warning letters) within the 'harder' forms of enforcement, some chose not to on the assumed premise that drug addicts are too chaotic to take heed of such measures. Our research indicated that such 'steps' in escalating enforcement strategies can act as an effective deterrent to participating in street activity for a number of street users and/or motivate them to make positive lifestyle changes – sometimes quite unexpectedly.

Enforcement initiatives are articulated in a coherent and positive manner

According to a number of support providers, the potential utility of enforcement measures, particularly ASBOs, is diminished if they are articulated in a purely punitive manner – as this frequently causes street users to feel that 'everyone is against them' and all too often engenders a counterproductive response. On the other hand, enforcement interventions can be used as a tool to help 'lever' street users towards support services and/or a reduction in the damaging aspects of their lifestyle if enforcement agents and support workers communicate a clear, consistent message emphasising support options available and identifying a positive path for the future. As one outreach worker reported, the serving of an ASBO (or implementation of another enforcement measure) can provide an opportunity to say to a street user:

> "'Right, what are we going to do about this? Do you want to go to prison or do you want to try and change things? This is just a bit of paper, it's not the end of the world. You still have control.'" (frontline worker, Brighton)

Impact of personal circumstances

A number of findings emerged regarding the characteristics of street users and their personal circumstances wherein enforcement appears *more* or *less* likely to lead to positive lifestyle changes. Again it must be stressed that the following points are not intended to be 'deterministic' or prescriptive, but they do represent what our data indicates are the key factors that heighten or diminish the chances of positive or negative outcomes.

Enforcement is most likely to 'work' for street users who ...

...have had some experience of stability

Support providers emphasised that enforcement was more likely to be successful with those street users who have had experience of stability at some point in their lives:

> 'Clients who've had busy successful lives that fell apart because of drug misuse becoming out of control are relatively easy to get back on track.' (support provider, Southwark)

> 'There was a chap who was a habitual beggar in Birmingham city centre.... He's an educated lad, really well-educated lad, fallen on – for whatever personal reasons

he'd ended up in this situation.... All of a sudden he was getting arrested all the time.... He was thinking "What the hell am I doing with my life?", went back to his dad who he hadn't spoken to in however many years, got himself off the drugs, and he's now back in college and got a full-time job.' (police representative, Birmingham)

...have something positive to return or aspire to

A closely related point is that enforcement is more likely to be effective when a street user has something tangible to look forward to, that is, something to motivate them to maintain positive lifestyle changes. This typically concerned re-establishing relations with family members:

'I just gotta get my life back on track, back to see my family again.' (street user, Birmingham)

The parent–child bond seemed the predominant concern for street users, rather than, say, re-establishing relations with spouses or partners:

'Before when I first started taking drugs and drinking and everything I didn't feel no self-worth, I didn't think I was worth it. But now I think to myself I've got a little girl ... so I can't go out there and kill myself or inject and drink myself to death like because I've got to be a role model to her.' (street user, Southwark)

...have recent experience of other 'crisis points'

Street users often emphasised that these 'internal' factors were more important in prompting them to address their addictions than external (coercive) interventions (see Chapter 3), but enforcement action could, especially if it followed recent experiences of such 'crisis points', operate as an additional motivating factor prompting them to make positive changes in their lives.

'I'd had enough of it, I'm getting too old, that's my reason [for wanting to change]. Fed up of it, fed up of taking drugs.... I started being ill. My chest, you know, oh, everything sort of come down at once, I felt ill, I felt drained, depressed, oh man.... You just get tired of it.... And I've had enough.... I want to live a normal life like everybody else.' (street user, Westminster)

Enforcement is least likely to 'work' for street users who ...

...have a long history of street living and/or substance misuse

The process of motivating a street user to alter their lifestyle – including through enforcement interventions – is particularly difficult with those who have no experience of the stability (or 'normality') that mainstream society expects them to aspire to:

'[Enforcement initiatives] may pull [some people] short and make them think "What the fuck am I doing, what am I getting myself into?"... But for people who've been misusing substances for 15, 20 years, in and out of hostels, on and off the streets, travelling around the country, they're just not effective. It's harder for those people.' (support provider, Brighton)

Drug workers suggest that the age at which people start using illicit drugs is an especially important factor:

> 'Some of our clients have been using Class A drugs since age 11, 12, and are now 40, so leaving that lifestyle will involve changing every aspect of their lives. This is 'normality' for them.' (frontline worker, Brighton)

Such individuals, as Buchanan (2004, p 393) has commented 'need social *integration* not reintegration ... *habilitation* not rehabilitation' (emphasis added).

...have experienced extreme trauma

Some street users had had such traumatic life histories that enforcement had, relatively speaking, a minor impact on them:

> 'For a lot of our clients they've been through that much crap in their lives that the "stick" isn't that hard compared to some of the other stuff that they've been through. And that's why the stick doesn't make much difference.' (frontline worker, Westminster)

...feel that the alternatives available are worse than street living

Many street users do not perceive the alternatives to a street lifestyle as preferable, particularly if they have had negative experiences in homeless hostels or have suffered the boredom and isolation that is so commonly experienced after resettlement:

> 'I didn't have any friends that didn't use and it was a case of either go out and use with your friends or stay indoors and do nothing. And I thought well what's the point of getting clean if you ain't doing nothing, locking yourself away?' (street user, Brighton)

...have inadequately treated mental health problems

Support providers questioned the degree to which some street users can exercise an 'informed choice' about their involvement in street culture activities and response to enforcement initiatives given the widespread failure to adequately diagnose and treat mental health problems among the street population. Support providers generally argued (and many enforcement agents accepted) that 'harder' forms of enforcement can set such street users on a path towards almost inevitable 'failure':

> 'Where ASBOs don't work at all – and it has at times been farcical – has been those people with mental health problems.... They were giving ASBOs to people who really didn't know what they meant. And that's where I really do draw the line on the whole ASBO thing.... Some of these younger drug users that were just hanging around doing nothing, some of the impetus of the ASBO has motivated them to change, but then they have the capability of doing it.... A lot of the people we're working with are not capable of making those sort of changes and never will be. Let's be realistic about that.' (support provider, Leeds)

...have particularly severe or 'chaotic' substance misuse problems

Street users with 'chaotic' heroin and, especially, crack habits can find it difficult to focus on anything other than the source of their next 'fix' (Tyler, 1995; see also Davies and Waite, 2004), meaning that they rarely engage proactively with interventions of any kind. There were similar, and possibly worse, difficulties engaging those who had the most severe alcohol problems (see also Segal, 1991):

> 'Some of our guys are too far gone. I can think of one who honestly wouldn't know if he's on an ASBO or not. No idea, he's so far gone on the drink. ASBO, shmasbo.' (frontline worker, Southwark)

Street users with Korsakoff's syndrome perhaps represent the most extreme example, wherein physical damage to their brain caused by long-term alcoholism renders them incapable of comprehending either the impact of their actions on the community or the consequences of failing to adhere to restrictions imposed on street activity (see, for example, Wilhite, 1992; Lehman et al, 1993; also Spence et al, 2004). Related to this, one support provider provided a cogent account of the divergent impacts of escalating enforcement interventions on some of his 'ASBO'd' clients:

> 'A and B ... ran it to the last but they're both compos mentis adults.... So although they'll still have the odd drink on the Green they are really playing it cautiously and the chances of them being nicked and ending up in a prison are quite slim because they are responding to that pressure. And it has altered their behaviour. It hasn't stopped them being ... heavy drinkers, but it has made them a bit more receptive to offers of support and interventions. Whereas the two people who have been imprisoned, X and Y, I think they've both got problems understanding what's going on. X we think [has] got some sort of organic brain damage, possibly Korsakoff's from heavy drinking. He doesn't get it.' (support provider, Southwark)

...already have an extensive criminal record

While there were a number of exceptions, support providers and enforcement agents typically found that the deterrent effect of enforcement interventions was severely weakened with street users who already had substantial experience of the criminal justice system. Prison holds little fear for many of these individuals, particularly those who are street homeless and consider themselves to have 'little to lose':

> 'For a lot of people like that, they're really not that fussed whether they're in prison or out. It's like "Mate you're going back to prison", "Oh, okay then." For someone like that an ASBO isn't going to work, is it?' (frontline worker, Brighton)

...are particularly 'authority averse' or 'anti establishment'

It was not uncommon for some of the more 'entrenched' or 'difficult' street users to exhibit symptoms of what a number of support providers referred to as 'fuck you syndrome'. These street users failed to comprehend that it was aspects of their *behaviour* that were causing offence and leading to enforcement; rather, they perceived themselves to be victims of a targeted personal vendetta by enforcement agencies and/or mainstream society. Such perceptions were reinforced by the discretionary nature of street drinking bans, in particular.

...consider themselves to be 'hopeless cases'

Some street users explained that they were unresponsive to either enforcement or supportive interventions because they considered themselves to be 'beyond help'. They had lost all hope of ever being able to change, a view often borne out of previous post-treatment relapses and/or barriers encountered when attempting to access appropriate support (see also Allen et al, 2003):

> 'They kept asking me if I wanted treatment and it was like "I've been there and done that and it don't work, not for me".... I'd resigned myself to the fact that I was going to be found dead in a car park somewhere.' (street user, Brighton)

Conclusions

In a minority of the cases we encountered, harder forms of enforcement – particularly ASBOs – did appear to have contributed to significant positive life changes for street users (for example, increased engagement with support services). Thus, our evidence indicates that there is a role for (carefully managed) enforcement in attempts to improve the circumstances of some vulnerable street users, including some of those most firmly enmeshed in street lifestyles. However, the unpredictability of street users' responses to enforcement, coupled with the very real possibility of significant negative impacts for some, makes enforcement action a 'high risk' strategy with regards to the well-being of street users. That said, while it is not possible to predict with any certainty when enforcement will and will not lead to beneficial outcomes for specific street users, we can identify both (a) policy and practice conditions conducive to positive outcomes; and (b) personal characteristics and circumstances of street users that apparently make them *more* or *less* likely to respond in positive ways to enforcement. If taken into account within enforcement strategies, these considerations will minimise, although not eliminate, the risk of harm to vulnerable street users by enforcement action.

6

Conclusions and policy implications

Introduction

This study set out to examine the impact of a range of enforcement interventions on the welfare of street users in England, and to identify the circumstances associated with any particular positive and negative impacts. Street users were defined as all those involved in rough sleeping, begging and street drinking (and we also considered the specific experiences of people selling *The Big Issue*). The research further sought to take into account the impact of enforcement action with street users on other stakeholders in the community, in particular local residents and businesses.

Detailed, qualitative case studies were undertaken in five locations across England, selected to represent different geographical contexts where street culture activities were viewed as a significant problem, and where diverse enforcement approaches were being pursued. The selected case study areas were:

- Westminster
- Southwark
- Birmingham
- Leeds
- Brighton

This final chapter summarises the conclusions of the study and the policy implications that arise from it.

Conclusions

This study confirmed the findings of previous research that those involved in street activities were highly vulnerable individuals: almost all street users encountered had (or had recently experienced) serious drug, alcohol and/or mental health problems, and the great majority had suffered a traumatic childhood. All of the in-depth interviewees were homeless[8] or had a history of homelessness.

---

[8]   That is, they were sleeping rough or were living in temporary or insecure forms of accommodation, such as hostels, night shelters, squats, or were 'sofa surfing' round friends' and relatives' houses.

It was mainly local rather than national pressures that led to a shift towards the use of enforcement in the case study areas. Street activities, particularly begging and street drinking in large groups, were perceived by local residents and business to have had a very negative impact on concentrated areas within each of the case studies. Problems were particularly pronounced in neighbourhoods characterised by a concentration of support services, a built environment conducive to street lifestyles, and proximity to illicit street drug markets and/or begging opportunities. However, central government provided both the encouragement for, and the 'tools' to enable, action to be taken to combat 'problematic street culture'. Affected members of the public, and enforcement agents, were not unsympathetic to the vulnerability of street users, but were clear that their top priority was a reduction in the negative impact of street culture on their daily lives.

The tools employed ranged from 'hard' forms of enforcement (such as ASBOs and arrests), through to 'softer' forms (particularly controlled drinking zones, alternative giving schemes and designing out environmental measures). The degree to which these measures were accompanied by supportive interventions was highly variable across the case studies. In some areas carefully coordinated support packages were integral to enforcement strategies; in others, enforcement and supportive interventions were employed virtually independently of one another.

Each case study area adopted a combination of enforcement measures that, together, had resulted in a sharp decline in street activities in virtually all of the targeted 'hotspots'. Some of the softer forms of enforcement – especially controlled drinking zones and environmental measures such as hot-washing – were highly effective in reducing the visibility of street activities. However, such measures rarely provided any discernible benefits for street users themselves.

Harder forms of enforcement – particularly ASBOs – were also key to the reduction of street activities in targeted areas given their powerful (direct and indirect) deterrent effect. While far fewer ASBOs had actually been issued to street users than was commonly supposed, it was clear that even the threat of an ASBO could bring about substantial changes in street behaviour because of the possibility of long prison sentences for breach of ASBO conditions. Moreover, when preceded by warning stages (such as ABCs or ABAs), and integrated with intensive supportive interventions, harder measures such as ASBOs could bring about positive benefits for some street users, causing them to desist from ASB and engage with drug treatment and other services. Enforcement in these instances acted as a 'crisis point' prompting reflection and change.

However, enforcement (in both its hard and soft forms) clearly led to 'geographical displacement' (relocation of street activities), and, in London especially, there were concerns about a 'lowest common denominator' effect, whereby if one council takes a hard stance against street culture neighbouring authorities potentially feel obliged to do likewise. There was also consistent evidence of 'activity displacement', wherein street users turned to shoplifting or sex work during 'begging clampdowns' in order to generate the funds required for their drug and/or alcohol problem.

While it is impossible to predict with certainty what the outcomes of enforcement will be for a given individual or group, it is clear that the impact depends to a significant degree on the manner in which enforcement is implemented, especially whether there is appropriate interagency working and support integrated with enforcement interventions. Also crucial are the personal circumstances of an individual street user: for example, street users seemed more likely to respond positively to enforcement if they had had experience of stability at some point in their lives, had something positive to return or aspire to, and/ or had recent experience of other 'crisis points' (such as an overdose scare, or the death of a friend) that had prompted them to contemplate their lifestyle and future. Conversely, street users seemed less likely to benefit from enforcement if, for example, they had a long history of street living and/or substance misuse, had inadequately treated mental health problems, had particularly severe or chaotic substance misuse problems, already had an extensive criminal record, or considered themselves to be 'hopeless cases'.

Given the unpredictability of outcomes for specific street users, and the potential for very negative impacts for some (for example, diversion into more dangerous activities/spaces as well as the possibility of lengthy prison sentences), enforcement is undoubtedly a *high risk* strategy with regards to the well-being of street users.

National and local policy implications

Based on our examination of enforcement action and impacts in these five locations across England, a number of policy implications can be highlighted for central government and local practitioners (both enforcement agents and support providers).

- Gaps within local service networks need to be addressed, not only to increase the likelihood of successful resettlement and treatment of drug or alcohol addictions, but also to enhance the incentive for street users to move away from lifestyles that are damaging to themselves and, sometimes, to the local community. While access to drug treatment has improved significantly in many areas in recent years, provision of alcohol treatment services remains inadequate, and the availability of appropriate treatment for mental health problems is frequently poor. Moreover, further research is required into the efficacy of coercive drug and alcohol treatment – particularly as employed with vulnerable street users – as this remains a matter of acute controversy.
- The specific actions and personal circumstances of street users must be taken into account in making a considered judgement on whether enforcement action is both necessary and likely to be effective in each particular case. 'Blanket' approaches, to pursue enforcement against all street users engaged in a particular activity, especially where the views of support providers are not taken into account, are likely to have a very negative impact on at least some members of this group, many of whom are highly vulnerable.
- Given the potential for serious negative impacts on the well-being of street users, 'harder' enforcement measures (for example, ASBOs) should only be used as a last resort, when a street user persistently refuses to engage with supportive interventions and continues exhibiting ASB. They should never be used with extremely vulnerable street users, particularly those with serious mental health problems or conditions such as Korsakoff's syndrome. Such individuals are unable to comprehend or respond constructively to enforcement action, and it is likely to exacerbate their already difficult circumstances, while at the same time bringing no discernable benefits to the wider community.
- For enforcement to have a reasonable prospect of prompting a positive response from any street users, it must always be carefully integrated with individually tailored and (immediately) accessible supportive interventions; involve effective interagency working; and be articulated in such a way as to emphasise the positive options open to a street user, particularly the availability of appropriate accommodation and support.
- All relevant support providers should be represented at interagency operational forums to safeguard the well-being of vulnerable street users and ensure that supportive interventions are tailored appropriately to meet their needs. The Target and Tasking model employed in some of our case study areas appeared particularly effective at enabling this process. It is imperative, however, that frontline support workers are not implicated in any decision to pursue enforcement with a street user given the potential risk of damage to their working relationship with clients.

- Where harder forms of enforcement such as ASBOs are employed, 'warning' stages such as ABCs (or equivalent measures) should be used, as these have been shown to be effective in obviating the need for a full ASBO to be pursued in many instances.

- The behavioural and geographical prohibitions within ASBOs (or civil injunctions, where these are used) should be limited to those demonstrably necessary to address the specific anti-social actions of that particular individual, which are having a serious impact on the local community and cannot be appropriately addressed through the existing criminal law or other available means. In particular, ASBOs should not prohibit serious criminal acts or other matters unrelated to the anti-social street activities that the Order is primarily intended to prevent, nor should they be so widely drawn as to seriously impinge on the street user's quality of life or to make it almost inevitable that they will be breached.

- Guidelines to magistrates on what constitutes appropriate evidence of 'harassment, alarm or distress' in the context of begging, and, more generally, on sentencing for breach of ASBOs, would be very helpful.

- The arrest of people for simply sleeping rough should be avoided as this is of dubious legality, and was widely condemned by street users, support providers and the public alike. Fining people for sleeping rough and/or begging were entirely counterproductive measures with no discernible benefit to the community or street users.

- While the local community viewed controlled drinking zones (DPPOs) as highly effective, they lacked legitimacy in the eyes of street users and service providers because of the discretionary way in which they were policed. This is likely to remain the case unless controlled drinking zones are recast to affect all in the community *equally* (that is, to remove their 'discretionary' nature). Similarly, geographical displacement of street drinking is likely to remain commonplace unless these measures are complemented with supportive interventions. It is also necessary to challenge the 'logic' of street drinking by, for example, considering whether it is possible to provide appropriate alternative locations for alcoholic street drinkers to drink.

- Local authorities and service providers should think carefully before introducing alternative giving schemes. While they may serve to educate the public about the practice of begging, they do little to dissuade the public from giving directly to people who beg.

- Local authorities and others engaged in environmental measures to design out street culture must take cognisance of the likelihood of geographical displacement unless such measures are integrated with appropriate supportive interventions, as exemplified by the constructive hotspot closure approach.

- There was a clear value attached by enforcement agents, support providers and street users alike to dedicated street population policing teams. Consideration should be given to the introduction of these teams wherever there are significant concerns about street culture, and certainly where there are plans to introduce an enforcement agenda.

References

Adler, M., Bromley, C. and Rosie, M. (2000) 'Begging as a challenge to the welfare state', in R. Jowell, J. Curtice, A. Park and K. Thomson (eds) *British social attitudes: The 17th report 2000/2001*, London: Sage Publications.

Adriaenssens, S. and Cle, A. (2006) 'Beggars in Brussels or the globalisation of extreme poverty', Paper presented at the Dag van de Sociologe, Tilburg, 8 June.

Alcohol Concern (2001) *Wernicke-Korsakoff's syndrome*, London: Alcohol Concern.

Allen, C., Sprigings, N. and Kyng, E. (2003) *Street crime and drug misuse in Greater Manchester*, London: Home Office.

Arlington Housing Association (1992) *Homelessness and street drinking*, Arlington: Arlington Housing Association.

Ballantyne, S. (1999) *Unsafe streets: Street homelessness and crime*, London: IPPR.

Bowers, K.J. and Johnson, S.D. (2003) 'Measuring the geographical displacement and diffusion of benefit effects of crime prevention activity', *Journal of Quantitative Criminology*, vol 19, pp 275-301.

Buchanan, J. (2004) 'Missing links? Problem drug use and social exclusion', *Probation Journal*, vol 51, pp 387-97.

Camden Marketing (2004) *Your kindness could kill: Campaign evaluation report*, London: Camden Marketing.

Carver, J.A. (2004) 'Drug testing: a necessary prerequisite for treatment and for crime control', in P. Bean and T. Nemitz (eds) *Drug treatment: What works?*, London: Routledge, pp 142-77.

Checinski, K. and Ghodse, H. (2004) 'Types of treatment for types of patients', in P. Bean and T. Nemitz (eds) *Drug treatment: What works?*, London: Routledge.

Crime Reduction (2006) www.crimereduction.gov.uk/alcoholorders09.htm (21/8/2006).

Danczuk, S. (2000) *Walk on by... Begging, street drinking and the giving age*, London: Crisis.

Davies, R. and Waite, S. (2004) *Drugs use and begging: A practice guide*, London: Home Office.

Eick, V. (2003) 'New strategies of policing the poor: Berlin's neo-liberal security system', *Policing and Society*, vol 13, pp 365-79.

Farabee, D., Prendergast, P. and Anglin, D. (1998) 'The effectiveness of coerced treatment for drug-abusing offenders', *Federal Probation*, vol 62, pp 3-10.

Fischer, P.J. (1992) 'The criminalization of homelessness', in M.J. Robertson and M. Greenblatt (eds) *Homelessness: A national perspective*, New York, NY: Plenum Press, pp 57-64.

Fitzpatrick, S. and Jones, A. (2005) 'Pursuing social justice or social cohesion? Coercion in street homelessness policies in England', *Journal of Social Policy*, vol 34, pp 389-406.

Fitzpatrick, S. and Kennedy, C. (2000) *Getting by: Begging, rough sleeping and The Big Issue in Glasgow and Edinburgh*, Bristol/York: The Policy Press/Joseph Rowntree Foundation.

Fitzpatrick, S., Kemp, P. and Klinker, S. (2000) *Single homelessness: An overview of research in Britain*, Bristol/York: The Policy Press/Joseph Rowntree Foundation.

Fooks, G. and Pantazis, C. (1999) 'The criminalisation of homelessness, begging and street living', in P. Kennett and A. Marsh (eds) *Homelessness: Exploring the new terrain*, Bristol: The Policy Press, pp 123-59.

Gregoire, T.K. and Burke, A.C. (2004) 'The relationship of legal coercion to readiness to change among adults with alcohol or other drug problems', *Journal of Substance Abuse Treatment*, vol 26, pp 35-41.

Hermer, J. (1999) 'Policing compassion: "diverted giving" on the Winchester High Street', in H. Dean (ed) *Begging questions: Street-level economic activity and social policy failure*, Bristol: The Policy Press, pp 203-18.

Home Office (2002) *Together tackling anti-social behaviour: Action plan*, London: Home Office.

Home Office (2003) *A guide to Anti-social Behaviour Orders and Acceptable Behaviour Contracts*, London: Home Office.

Home Office (2004) *Perceptions of anti-social behaviour: Summary of the first stage of the three-year study commissioned by the Home Office Anti-Social Behaviour* Unit, London: Home Office.

Jane Walker Consultancy Ltd (2005) *Camberwell Street Drinking Intervention: An evaluation of the process and outcomes*, London: Safer Southwark Partnership.

Jowett, S., Banks, G., Brown, A. and Goodall, G. (2001) *Looking for change: The role and impact of begging on the lives of people who beg*, London: RSU/DTLR.

Lehman, L.B., Pilich, A. and Andrews, N. (1993) 'Neurological disorders resulting from alcoholism', *Alcohol Health and Research World*, vol 17, pp 305-9.

Longshore, D., Prendergast, M.L. and Farabee, D. (2004) 'Coerced treatment for drug-using criminal offenders', in P. Bean and T. Nemitz (eds) *Drug treatment – What works?*, London: Routledge, pp 110-22.

Maguire, M. (2002) 'Crime statistics: the "data explosion" and its implications', in M. Maguire, R. Morgan and R. Reiner (eds) *The Oxford handbook of criminology* (3rd edn), Oxford: Oxford University Press, pp 322-75.

Malinas, D (2004) 'No to the moving sidewalk: homeless mobilization against eviction, Shinjuku 1996', Paper presented at Asian Studies Conference Japan, Ichigaya Campus of Sophia University, June.

Marlowe, D.B. (2001) 'Coercive treatment of substance abusing criminal offenders', *Journal of Forensic Psychology Practice*, vol 1, pp 65-73.

May, J., Cloke, P. and Johnsen, S. (2005) 'Re-phasing neoliberalism: New Labour and Britain's crisis of street homelessness', *Antipode*, vol 37, pp 703-29.

MHF (Mental Health Foundation) (1996) *Too many for the road*, Report of the MHF Expert Working Group on persistent street drinkers, London: MHF.

Millie, A., Jacobson, J., McDonald, E. and Hough, M. (2005) *Anti-social behaviour strategies: Finding a balance*, Bristol/York: The Policy Press/Joseph Rowntree Foundation.

Mitchell, D. (1997) 'The annihilation of space by law: the roots and implications of anti-homeless laws in the United States', *Antipode*, vol 29, pp 303-36.

Nagel, T. (1986) *The view from nowhere*, Oxford: Oxford University Press.

National Coalition for the Homeless (2004) *Illegal to be homeless: The criminalisation of homelessness in the United States*, Washington, DC: National Coalition for the Homeless.

ODPM (Office of the Deputy Prime Minister) (1999) *Coming in from the cold: The government's strategy on rough sleeping*, London: ODPM.

Pawson, R. and Tilley, N. (1997) *Realistic evaluation*, London: Sage Publications.

Pleace, N. and Quilgars, D. (1996) *Health and homelessness in London*, London: King's Fund.

Prochaska, J.O. and Vellicer, W.F. (1997) 'The transtheoretical model of health behaviour change', *American Journal of Health Promotion*, vol 12, pp 38-48.

Prochaska, J.O., DiClemente, C.C., Velicer, W.F., Ginpil, S. and Norcross, J.C. (1985) 'Predicting change in smoking status for self-changers', *Addictive Behaviours*, vol 10, pp 395-406.

Randall, G. and Brown, S. (2002) *Helping rough sleepers off the streets: A report to the Homelessness Directorate*, London: ODPM.

Randall, G. and Brown, S. (2006) *Steps off the street: Solutions to street homelessness*, London: Crisis.

Segal, B.M. (1991) 'Homelessness and drinking: a study of a street population', *Drugs and Society*, vol 5, pp 1-136.

Shimwell, K. (1999) *Street substance use and homelessness in Rotherham*, Rotherham: Rotherham Community Alcohol Service.

Snow, D. and Mulcahy, M. (2001) 'Space, politics and the survival strategies of the homeless', *American Behavioural Scientist*, vol 45, pp 149-69.

Spence, S., Stevens, R. and Parks, R. (2004) 'Cognitive dysfunction in homeless adults: a systematic review', *Journal of the Royal Society of Medicine*, vol 97, pp 375-9.

Turning Point (2005) *The crack report*, London: Turning Point.

Tyler, A. (1995) *Street drugs*, London: Hodder and Stoughton.

Vision 21 (2001) *Time for change: A study of street drinking and begging in Camden and Islington*, London: Vision 21.

Wardhaugh, J. (1996) '"Homeless in Chinatown": deviance and social control in cardboard city', *Sociology*, vol 30, pp 701-16.

West, R. (2006) *Theory of addiction*, Oxford: Blackwell.

Wilhite, J. (1992) 'Public policy and the homeless alcoholic', in M.J. Robertson and M. Greenblatt (eds) *Homelessness: A national perspective*, New York, NY: Plenum Press, pp 187-96.

Appendix A:
Fieldwork conducted

Westminster

Enforcement agents
In-depth interviews with four enforcement agents

Support providers
In-depth interviews with eight support providers

Focus group with four support providers

Street users
In-depth interviews with nine street users

Focus group with six street users

Local residents and business proprietors
Focus group with four local residents

Other
Accompanied street outreach workers on one of their usual rounds, talking informally with street users en route

Southwark

Enforcement agents
In-depth interviews with four enforcement agents

Support providers
In-depth interviews with seven support providers

Focus group with four support providers

Street users
In-depth interviews with 10 street users

Focus group with 10 street users

Local residents and business proprietors
Focus group with 17 community representatives (including business proprietors, community council representatives, councillors etc)

Other

Attendance at Operations Forum meeting

Brighton

Enforcement agents
In-depth interviews with four enforcement agents

Support providers
In-depth interviews with two support providers

Three focus groups with a total of 13 support providers

Street users
In-depth interviews with six street users

Focus group with five street users

Local residents and business proprietors
In-depth interviews with three residents and business proprietors

Other
Attendance at two ASB casework meetings

Accompanied police officer on city centre beat

Leeds

Enforcement agents
In-depth interviews with three enforcement agents

Support providers
In-depth interviews with five support providers

Street users
In-depth interviews with six street users

Focus group with four street users (and two support providers)

Local residents and business proprietors
In-depth interviews with three business proprietors

Birmingham

Enforcement agents
In-depth interviews with seven enforcement agents

Support providers
In-depth interviews with seven support providers

Two focus groups with a total of eight support providers

Street users
In-depth interviews with five street users plus one 'vicarious' interview (written by a street user specifically for this project and passed on, with the street user's consent, by a support worker)

Focus group with four street users

Camden

Enforcement agents and support providers
Focus group with two enforcement agents and one support provider

Appendix B:
Interview topic guides

Topic guide 1: Street users

1. General background

- Ask name, age and where living at the moment.
- Where were you brought up as a child? Any experience of care? How did you get on at school? Did you get any qualifications when you left? What did you do when you left school?
- Are you working just now? What jobs/training/education have you had?
- Have you ever been married/cohabited? Have you any children?

2. Housing/homelessness history

- Have you always lived in this area? Have you moved around much? Why go/come back/move here?
- Have you ever been homeless? [probe definition of homelessness. Prompt on hostels/ night centres/staying care-of/squatting, etc] When/where/how long for?
- Have you ever slept rough? When/where/how long for? Why did/do you sleep rough?
- What type of accommodation would you like now? If no longer homeless, how did you manage to move on? [probe impact of interventions]

3. Health/personal history

- Do you have any health problems – physical/mental? When did they start/what caused them? Have they got anything to do with being homeless/roofless (where appropriate)?
- Do you drink/take drugs? Does it cause problems in your life? When/why did you become dependent on drink/drugs? [probe whether before/after homelessness] Would you like to stop/reduce or happy as you are? Have you had treatment? [probe type/ intensity]
- Have you ever been in trouble with the police/in prison/on remand? Have you ever been in psychiatric hospital/other long-stay medical care? Have you ever been in the armed forces?

4. Street life

- Is there much rough sleeping/begging/*Big Issue* vending/street drinking/street drugs/ street sex work around here? Overlap in people involved? Are numbers involved increasing/decreasing? Characteristics – gender; age; ethnic backgrounds? Are there distinct groups – new arrivals/long established; vulnerable/'professional beggars' etc?
- Have you ever begged? Have you ever asked people in the street for money?
- Have you ever sold *The Big Issue*?
- Have you been involved in street drinking?
- Have you been involved in street drugs scene – using/dealing?
- Have you ever had sex in exchange for money/food/drugs/somewhere to stay?

For each activity involved in:

- When did you start? Why? How often/in what circumstances do you do this? [probe link with homelessness/rooflessness; drug/alcohol use]
- How much money do you make from [activity] (where appropriate)? Does it have any advantages over other ways of getting money? Is it an alternative to social security/ crime/other [activities] for you, or do you still need these sources to get by?
- How do the public react to you when involved in activity? What contact with police/ homelessness other agencies when involved in [activity]?
- Do you engage in [activity] alone or with other people? Do you share your money/help each other? Any problems with other 'street people'/people taking advantage of you/ others on the street?
- Would you like to stop [activity] or prefer to carry on as you are? What would help you to stop? If you have stopped, how did you manage to do that?
- Do you think people should be allowed to engage in [activity] or something should be done to stop it?

5. Interventions

- Do you have a social worker/key worker/outreach worker/drugs worker/other support from agencies? Have you had these forms of help in the past? How often do they see you? How do you feel about them? How do they help you? Could they do more? What have been the most/least helpful agencies you have had contact with?
- Have you ever had an ASBO/injunction/arrest/DTTO/de-canning/moving on etc action taken against you? Can you take me through what happened? [probe process]
- What is your understanding of why this [enforcement action] was taken? What agencies were involved? How did you feel about it at the time (fair/unfair)? How do you feel about it now?
- What impact did it have on you – positive or negative? Did it change your behaviour/ attitudes/motivation in any way? [probe for anger/helplessness/heightened readiness to change/internalisation of external pressure] Did it have any impact on your housing situation; drug/alcohol use; involvement in crime, begging, sex work, etc? [probe for any geographical or activity displacement] How long did these changes last? Would it have had a different impact on you if you had had different housing, dependency, personal, etc circumstances at the time?
- Did you get any support before/during this [enforcement action]? What agencies helped/ supported you? Did this combination of help/enforcement make a difference? Were they at the right time/in the right order? Anything missing? What should they have done instead? What do you think would have happened if [enforcement action] hadn't have been taken?
- What about other people involved in [activity]? Will support/enforcement/combination tend to work best? When will and won't something work for most 'street people'?

- Are most 'street people' you know aware of ASBOs, DTTOs, etc? Has it made any difference to the behaviour/attitudes of those who haven't directly experienced them?
- Do you know about [diverted giving scheme] or [street drinking ban] in your area? What effect has this had on you/other 'street people'? [probe any evidence of displacement in geography/activity] Do you think it's fair/unfair? Why/why not? What should be done instead?

6. The future

- What is the most important thing that would make your life better just now?
- Hopes/fears for the future?
- Anything else you think we should know?

Thank for help.

Topic guide 2: Key informants

1. Personal background

- Personal – job title/roles; professional background; how long in post.
- Agency – purpose, size, staffing, client group, etc (as appropriate).
- Degree/type of involvement in addressing local street culture/homelessness.

2. Perception of local 'street scene'

- Scale/nature of: rough sleeping; begging; street drinking; street prostitution; street drug use/dealing; *Big Issue* vending.
- Relationship between these activities/degree of overlap; extent to which those involved are 'homeless' (note: not just rough sleeping).
- Changes over time in scale/nature of these activities. Reasons for any changes. [probe whether linked to interventions]
- Characteristics of those involved – age; gender; localness/transience; any whose first language not English? Support needs – alcohol, drugs, mental health, social isolation etc.
- Distinctive groups among street users? – 'new arrivals' versus long-term/'entrenched'; vulnerable homeless people versus 'professional beggars'/exploitative individuals, and whether any movement between these groups.
- Impact on local community – residents, businesses, visitors, etc.

3. Nature of interventions

- Main interventions that have been used locally: preventative; supportive [prompt on outreach/streetwork; accommodation; resettlement support; specialist support with drugs, alcohol, mental health, etc]; enforcement [prompt on ASBOs, injunctions, diverted giving schemes, criminal sanctions, DTTOs, DPPOs/byelaws]
- How are interventions combined/linked? What is nature/extent of multiagency working? How is own agency involved?
- How are (all) interventions targeted? What are triggers for enforcement? How is decision made that enforcement action is appropriate? Who is enforcement focused on – 'new arrivals', 'entrenched' or 'professionals'?

- Origins of current policies/development over time – impetus, local 'champions', impact of local politics, impact of legislation/central government initiatives; degree of emphasis given to tackling 'street culture' as compared with other ASB priorities.

4. Effectiveness of interventions

- What has been the overall impact on local street culture of using enforcement/combined interventions?
- Views on effectiveness of specific interventions/combinations of interventions.
- Do some interventions work for some but not others/in certain circumstances and not others? What makes the difference? What are the patterns? What about the timing/ordering of different types of interventions?
- How would they assess whether an intervention has 'worked'? [probe – a reduction in 'problem' street behaviour; resettlement for homeless/vulnerable groups; reduced impacts on wider community, etc]
- Any unintended/unexpected consequences of interventions (positive or negative)? Any evidence of geographical or activity displacement?
- Has knowledge of ASBOs, DTTOs, injunctions etc permeated through the local street homeless population? Has it made any difference to the behaviour/attitudes of those who haven't directly experienced them?
- Is the balance between prevention/support and enforcement interventions appropriate? Why/why not? [probe their understanding of effectiveness/fairness]
- Anything more/else that should be done? Any mistakes that have been made?
- Their view on the perceptions of others as to whether policies working – other agencies; street users; wider community.

5. Further help

- Any data/reports/policy documents/other literature?
- Other key informers we should speak to?
- Can they help with access to those working directly with street users?
- Can they help with access to street users/homeless people?
- Feedback seminar.

Thank for help.

Topic guide 3: Wider community

1. Personal background

- Each participant's – name; where lives/works; nature of interest/concern in local street culture; nature of group that represent (eg residents' group, business forum, etc); any personal/group involvement in development of policy/initiatives.

2. Perceptions of local 'street scene'

- Scale/nature of: rough sleeping; begging; street drinking; street prostitution; street drug use/dealing; *Big Issue* vending.
- Perceptions of degree of overlap between these activities. Views on whether those involved are 'homeless'. How do they define 'homeless'?

- Perceptions of change over time in scale/nature or visibility of these activities. Reasons for any change? [probe whether linked to interventions]
- Perceptions of characteristics of those involved – age; gender; localness/transience; support needs; distinctive groups, etc.
- Impact of these activities on local community – residents, businesses, visitors, etc. What are key concerns? How high a priority as compared with other forms of ASB?
- Do these activities affect some people in community more than others? If so, who/why?
- Do some activities or groups of street people present a greater problem for the community than others? Who/why?

3. Interventions

- Probe awareness/knowledge/understanding of interventions that are used locally: preventative; supportive [prompt on outreach/streetwork; resettlement support; specialist support with drugs, alcohol, mental health, etc]; enforcement [prompt on ASBOs, injunctions, diverted giving schemes, criminal sanctions, DTTOs, DPPOs/byelaws, etc]
- Probe knowledge/understanding of targeting of interventions and triggers for enforcement.
- What do they think the overall impact has been of enforcement/combined interventions on level/nature of street culture in area?
- Views on effectiveness/appropriateness of specific interventions/combinations of interventions. Has anything in particular worked/not worked? Why?
- How would they assess whether an intervention has 'worked'? [probe – a reduction in 'problem' street behaviour; resettlement for homeless/vulnerable groups; reduced impacts on wider community, etc]
- Have they noticed any particular impacts of interventions (positive or negative)? Any concern about geographical or activity displacement?
- Do they think it is likely that some interventions work for some street users but not others/in certain circumstances and not others? What do they think is likely to make the difference?
- Do they think the balance between prevention/support and enforcement is appropriate? Why/why not? [probe their understandings of effectiveness/fairness]
- What are the general views of those they represent (where appropriate)?
- Anything different/more that should be done? Who should be responsible?

4. Conclude

- Outline reporting plans. Mention feedback seminar.

Thank for help.

Printed and bound by CPI Group (UK) Ltd, Croydon, CR0 4YY

14/04/2025

14656885-0001